"*Thinking Through Stories* strengthens the case for pre-college philosophy and shows us the value of picture books for engaging young children in philosophical discussion. In addition, Wartenberg offers sage advice about how to facilitate philosophical discussion with young children, especially when it comes to dealing with difficult topics. I highly recommend this book to any teacher who values children's native curiosity and is sensitive to their concerns."

Dr. Philip Cam, *Honorary Associate Professor at the School of Humanities and Languages, University of New South Wales. His most recent book is Philosophical Inquiry: Combining the Tools of Philosophy with Inquiry-based Teaching and Learning.*

"In this elegantly and clearly written book, Tom Wartenberg provides a compelling account of why children will benefit from doing philosophy and of the value of picture books in helping them to do so. Teachers and parents interested in doing philosophy with their children should read this book."

Berys Gaut and Morag Gaut, *authors of Philosophy for Young Children: A Practical Guide.*

"*Thinking Through Stories: Children, Philosophy, and Picture Books* significantly fills a gap in the K-12 philosophy literature. By emphasizing the role that picture books can play, Wartenberg accomplishes two important tasks. First, he demonstrates that not all philosophy needs to be done with arguments or words. Second, by focusing on the role that picture books can play in inspiring philosophical ideas, he expands the range of ages for children who can participate on their own terms, without, for example, someone needing to read a book to them. Wartenberg's approach provides greater autonomy to children who wish to participate in philosophical discussions and for that he should be deeply commended."

Claire Katz, *Professor of Philosophy and the Murray and Celeste Fasken Chair in Distinguished Teaching and Associate Dean of Faculties at Texas A & M University. She is the editor of Growing Up with Philosophy Camp.*

"*Thinking Through Stories* reflects on the Philosophy for/with Children movement at its 50-year mark. Weaving together theory and practice, Wartenberg contrasts different strands within the movement: picture books versus philosophical novels; philosophy as established canons of thought versus the embrace of wonder and perplexity. He offers insightful and practical advice for how to help children "think for themselves together" and underscores the Social and Emotional Learning to be gained through such joint inquiry. This is a must read for those new to the field and seasoned practitioners alike."

Dr. Erik Kenyon, *teaches Middle School Latin and Humanities at Friends Academy in Dartmouth, MA. He is co-author of Ethics for the Very Young: A Philosophy Curriculum for Early Childhood Education.*

"Thomas Wartenberg understands two things that are not widely enough appreciated. He knows that great children's books touch on profound themes and knows that kids, even quite young kids, are natural philosophers, eager to explore big ideas. *Thinking Through Stories* explains why it is important to help children learn to think philosophically and offers thoughtful advice about how to do so using children's books (especially picture books). Wartenberg also shows us how to deepen the experience of reading to children. The book offers a road map to joy for parents, teachers, and philosophers."

Sam Swope, *author of The Araboolies of Liberty Street, and founder of the Academy for Teachers.*

THINKING THROUGH STORIES

This book provides justification and instruction for exploring philosophy with children, especially by using picture books to initiate philosophical discussion. By demonstrating to teachers, and others that picture books often embed philosophical issues into their narratives, and that this makes picture books a natural place to go to help young children investigate philosophical issues, the author offers a straightforward approach to engaging young students. In particular, this volume highlights how philosophical dialogue enhances children's sense of self, provides a safe space for the discussion of issues that they are confronted with in living their lives, and develops an admirable method for resolving conflict that the children can use in other contexts.

Thomas E. Wartenberg is Professor of Philosophy Emeritus at Mount Holyoke College. He is the author of *Big Ideas for Little Kids: Teaching Philosophy Through Children's Literature* and *A Sneetch Is a Sneetch and Other Philosophical Discoveries: Finding Wisdom in Children's Literature*.

THINKING THROUGH STORIES

Children, Philosophy, and Picture Books

Thomas E. Wartenberg

Routledge
Taylor & Francis Group

NEW YORK AND LONDON

Cover image: DrAfter123 / Getty Images

First published 2022
by Routledge
605 Third Avenue, New York, NY 10158

and by Routledge
2 Park Square, Milton Park, Abingdon, Oxon, OX14 4RN

Routledge is an imprint of the Taylor & Francis Group, an informa business

Library of Congress Cataloging-in-Publication Data
Names: Wartenberg, Thomas E., author.
Title: Thinking through stories: children, philosophy, and picture books/
    Thomas E. Wartenberg.
Description: New York, NY: Routledge, 2022. | Includes bibliographical
    references and index.
Identifiers: LCCN 2021044131 (print) | LCCN 2021044132 (ebook) |
    ISBN 9781032190396 (hardback) | ISBN 9781032190389 (paperback) |
    ISBN 9781003257455 (ebook)
Subjects: LCSH: Philosophy and children. | Philosophy—Study and teaching
    (Elementary) | Picture books for children—Educational aspects. |
    Critical thinking in children.
Classification: LCC B105.C45 W37 2022 (print) |
    LCC B105.C45 (ebook) | DDC 108.3—dc23
LC record available at https://lccn.loc.gov/2021044131
LC ebook record available at https://lccn.loc.gov/2021044132

ISBN: 978-1-032-19039-6 (hbk)
ISBN: 978-1-032-19038-9 (pbk)
ISBN: 978-1-003-25745-5 (ebk)

DOI: 10.4324/9781003257455

Typeset in Bembo
by KnowledgeWorks Global Ltd.

For Jake

Who first showed me the way
with love and gratitude

CONTENTS

List of Figure   *xi*
Preface   *xii*

1 Introduction   1

PART I
The Case for Philosophy for/with Children   **9**

2 Why Teach Children Philosophy?   11

3 The Role of Wonder in Childhood   22

PART II
Why Picture Books?   **39**

4 The Uses and Limitations of Philosophical Novels   41

5 The Advantages of Picture Books   51

6 How Picture Books Actually Philosophize   61

PART III
**Issues about Facilitating Picture-Book
Philosophy Discussions** **73**

7 How Someone Who Doesn't Already Know
   Philosophy Can Teach It   75

8 Using Picture Books to Discuss Racial Issues   86

9 How to Facilitate Discussions of Books with Morals   99

10 Conclusion   107

Appendix: Glossary of Philosophical Terms and Names of Philosophers   *113*
Bibliography / Works Cited   *117*
Index   *120*

LIST OF FIGURE

7.1   Concept Map Diagram   77

PREFACE

All writing is a communal affair. Despite the isolation that is necessary to write a book, the activity is not as solitary as it is often taken to be. Anyone sitting down in front of their computer or pad of paper engages in an act of communication with real or imagined dialogue partners. The solitary activity of writing is inherently social.

Nowhere is this truer than in my work bringing philosophy into pre-college educational environments. From the beginning, others have always supported my efforts in this arena and encouraged me to expand them. My efforts to find words to explain the importance of bringing philosophy to young children and the best methods for doing so represent only the tip of the large iceberg most of which remains invisible, submerged.

So, let me here shine the light on some of those without whom my own efforts in this area might not have developed in the way that they did. First, without the support of Mary Cowhey, the teacher with whom I first introduced philosophical discussions of picture books into a classroom, I would never have had the courage to discuss philosophy with 5- and 6-year olds. The late Susan Fink was also supportive of my efforts from the beginning and welcomed me and my students into her classroom. Her passion for teaching and commitment to her students inspired all of us. Finally, Gwen Agna, the principal of the Jackson Street Elementary School in Northampton, MA, believed in my efforts and provided me with the support I needed to bring my ideas to fruition. Thanks to her support, I was able to work with Mary and Sue and bring my students to the school for philosophy discussions in all the elementary grades.

My good friend Lan Katz, the founder and first Executive Director of the Martin Luther King (MLK) Jr. School of Excellence in Springfield, MA, saw the potential that teaching philosophy to children would have for the students in his school. Since the second year of its existence, all the second graders at MLK have taken a philosophy class. Many aspects of my work in p4/wc were developed to help my students work with the students at MLK.

I have also enjoyed the support of a variety of different organizations. The Squire Family Foundation, through the auspices of its director Roberta Israeloff, provided me with a grant that enabled me to expand and develop my program, as well as to have the time to write my first book in this field, *Big Ideas for Little Kids*. I am very grateful for their support. PLATO, the Philosophy Learners and Teachers Organization, has also been an important source of support. I have served on the Board of PLATO and as its president. The biennial conferences of ICPIC, the International Council of Philosophical Inquiry with Children, have been a great venue for presenting my work.

I cannot list all of the conferences where I have presented my work or the schools at which I have given talks and workshops but I have been gratified by everyone who has been interested in my efforts and have learned a great deal from interacting with individuals who have been developing their own p4/wc programs.

I would like to thank Sondra Bachrach for supporting my application for a Fulbright Fellowship that brought me to Wellington, New Zealand in 2005, where I worked at the Island Bay School to develop a philosophy program there. I gave classes to two groups of students each week and held workshops for faculty. This experience enriched my understanding of doing philosophy with young children and introduced me to different approaches used in different countries. I was also able to visit various universities in New Zealand and Australia, and learned a great deal from all the practitioners in those countries.

This manuscript has also benefitted from the assistance of a number of people. Two practitioners of p4/wc and colleagues in PLATO, Erik Kenyon and Claire Katz, read the entire manuscript and gave me excellent advice. The three anonymous reviewers for Routledge also gave me valuable suggestions for improving the manuscript. My neighbor and Smith College Education Professor Rosetta Cohen gave me the impetus to write this book. Her comments on an essay I had intended for the journal she edits made me realize I needed to write a book to demonstrate the validity of my perspective. Without her suggestions and support, I would not have decided to write it.

As usual, my son Jake has been a source of support and inspiration for me. His innate philosophical curiosity first got me intrigued by the idea of discussing philosophical issues with a young child. He has also generously shared his technical skills with me, enabling me to keep working on this book despite power outages and computer failures.

Matthew Friberg, my editor at Routledge, has been unfailingly supportive of this project. He and all the others at Routledge deserve my thanks for helping to bring this book to fruition.

A word about the picture books I discuss in this book. As readers will undoubtedly notice, many of them are classics in the genre. I have chosen to use such books because they are well known to educators and widely available. They are also some of the most philosophical picture books I know of.

Sometimes, however, the topic I am discussing requires the use of more contemporary works. This is especially true in my discussion of teaching race in Chapter 7. There, I have incorporated recent books because they do a better job of presenting racial issues than some older books that people have used.

Anyone looking for suggestions about books to use for facilitating philosophical dialogues would do well to consult the website that I developed that is now managed by the Prindle Ethics Institute: teachingchildrenphilosophy. org. The site features over 300 picture books, both classic and contemporary. There are lists of books organized by the area of philosophy they can be used to discuss, making it easy for facilitators to find books about the issues they want to discuss with their students. This is a great resource that is the result of the efforts of many of my own students and those at other institutions who have contributed modules for many of the books. I am grateful to the Institute, in particular to Christiane Wisehart who oversaw the transfer, and to the Institute's director Andrew Cullison for their interest in and support of my work.

1
INTRODUCTION

When I was growing up in Great Neck, a suburb of New York City on Long Island, my parents would often take us to Manhattan as a special treat. We would drive the Long Island Expressway, often referred to sarcastically as the greatest parking lot in the world. Our route would take us through Queens where one cemetery followed another in a seemingly infinite sequence until we descended into semi-darkness of the Queens-Midtown Tunnel.

As a boy, I was terrified of those cemeteries, probably because they brought me face-to-face with the reality of death. As we drove past row after row of headstones and graves, I would slump onto the space between the front and rear seats of our family car, as if hiding there would somehow save me from the fate all those graves and their markers represented. Death was definitely something that freaked me out.

Perhaps surprisingly, my parents never commented on my odd behavior. I never discussed this with them while they were alive, so I don't know how they rationalized their decision not to talk with me about it. Even in religious school—I was brought up going to a reform Jewish synagogue and was eventually Bar Mitzvahed—I don't recall the subject of death ever coming up, which is odd given how central a role death plays in religion. The closest we ever came to discussing death in a meaningful way was to talk about why Jews did not believe in heaven, hell, or an afterlife.

Because no one ever discussed the significance of the fact that each of us will someday no longer exist, my fear of death festered without any outlet while I was growing up. It was not until I discovered philosophy as a high school student that I began to realize that death was a subject that philosophers had addressed throughout the ages. From Socrates' claim that the life of a

DOI: 10.4324/9781003257455-1

philosopher was simply preparation for death to Martin Heidegger's claim that human beings flee the awareness of their own mortality, philosophers have discussed death in ways that can be helpful for those trying to come to terms with this most fundamental and terrifying fact about human life. Just realizing that other people have had the same concerns that I did as a child was very helpful to me in dealing with my own anxiety.

Had I been brought up in a more enlightened environment, I might have taken part in an elementary-school dialogue about death, one that I would have found very reassuring. Discovering that everyone—all of my classmates included—was scared of dying and unsure of what happened after death would have been profoundly reassuring and healing to me: reassuring, because I would no longer have thought of myself as odd for worrying about dying; healing, because I would then have seen myself as sharing a fundamental concern with my school peers.

Maybe this is one reason why I have become such a passionate advocate for discussing philosophy with children. I see philosophical discussions as one important vehicle for communicating with children and allowing them to express their deepest fears, desires, and beliefs. And in so doing, children learn that they are not as different from their classmates as they had feared, for they all have experienced some "weird thoughts," such as "Could the world have just begun 5 minutes ago, with many false memories implanted in my brain?"

But the communication that takes place during philosophical dialogues does not just involve the expression of one's beliefs, though that is an important part of it. It requires that one *interact* with others who are similar to oneself. In this respect, philosophy is not a solitary enterprise, requiring lots of time spent by oneself reflecting about the nature of reality. Instead, philosophy as practiced in elementary schools is a *communal* activity in which a group of young people talk to one another, listen to what everyone else has to say, and critically evaluate the reasons the students give in support of their beliefs.

Too often, philosophers have ignored the communal nature of their enterprise. René Descartes, for example, begins his *Meditations on First Philosophy* by acknowledging the context for his meditative practice: he has withdrawn to the country so that he will not be distracted by urban life and can single-mindedly devote himself to determining which, if any, of his beliefs he can know with certainty. But even as he claimed that doing philosophy required him to isolate himself, Descartes actually distributed copies of his *Meditations* to the leading philosophers of his day, who responded with objections to which Descartes then offered replies. Hardly what one would expect if philosophy were truly a solitary affair.

Philosophy for and with children (p4/wc, hereafter)—I am here using the awkward label that many have adopted to refer to this field—stands firmly in a tradition that sees philosophy as a communal enterprise.[1] In so doing, p4/wc places itself into a philosophical tradition that can trace its lineage back at least to Baruch Spinoza who saw all of humanity as an aspect of a single, overarching entity which he characterized with the dual label, *Deus sive Natura*, God or Nature. More recently, the pragmatist tradition, inaugurated by Charles Sanders Peirce and developed by William James and John Dewey among others, posited philosophy as an activity requiring a group of people committed to engaging in a critical assessment of their most-cherished ideas.

With children, the group setting for philosophical dialogues is important for many reasons. As I have already mentioned, seeing that other children share one's own concerns can be a powerfully liberating experience for a child who thinks of themselves as having fears and desires that no one else shares. Noticing that others have similar concerns can lead a child to feel less odd and unusual, since the "odd" beliefs they have will come to be seen as indicative of their philosophical nature.

An individual child may find it hard to reflect upon the sorts of issues that are the lifeblood of philosophy. In a group setting, with other children vying to express their ideas, such a child will be able to learn from what they see the other children doing. Working together, the children can come to develop ideas that none of them would have thought of working on their own. To put it somewhat paradoxically, p4/wc teaches children to *think for themselves together*.

1.1 Why Don't We Teach Children Philosophy?

Given the naturalness of children's interest in discussing philosophical issues, it may be surprising to realize how infrequently philosophy is taught to pre-college students in the United States. Philosophy is often seen as the lynch pin of the humanities, anchoring the other humanistic disciplines such as literature, art, music, and the performing arts (theater, film, etc.). But unlike those other humanistic disciplines, philosophy is not one of the core subjects in the curricula of pre-college classes. While it is difficult to imagine an elementary school curriculum that did not include reading, writing, and art, the same cannot be said of philosophy. It is the rare school—other than religiously affiliated ones and those in the International Baccalaureate Program—that includes philosophy in its curriculum, especially for younger pre-college students.

Why is this so? One of the peculiarities of the Western philosophical tradition is its repeated insistence that philosophy is not a subject suitable for young people to study. Plato, the great Greek philosopher, argued in his dialogue, *The Republic*, that philosophy should only be studied by people toward the end of their lives, once they had been educated and pursued a career, thus not before the age of 50. In part, this was because he thought that a person could only do philosophy if they had already studied mathematics, literature, and other fields. Once a person had this background, they would be ready to embark on a philosophical education, but not before then.

We can understand why Plato believed young people should not be taught philosophy by situating this belief within Plato's overall conception of philosophy. Plato believed that the things that most of us take to be *real* in the course of living our lives, things like tables, chairs, and beds, are not fully real, for they are subject to change and destruction. True reality, Plato maintained, must be unchanging and eternal, and he dubbed the separate realm in which such realities existed as the world of *Forms*. The Forms were those ultimately real things, like Beauty and Truth that the *Appearances* in our world only approximate. Unlike the constantly changing things of this world, the Forms remain the same, so that the Form of Beauty will always be beautiful and never admit its opposite, say, ugliness.

Plato's general conception of philosophy is derived from this metaphysical view. While most people are only aware of the existence of ordinary things—*Appearances* in Plato's terminology—the task of philosophy is to articulate and understand the nature of the ultimate reality, the *Forms*. While we all are aware of beautiful things, from a porcelain bowl to a stunning sunset, philosophers have to learn how to become aware of the Forms. This is not something that happens naturally, for it requires training.

The training that philosophers need involves sharpening their ability to perceive abstract objects. Aside from the Forms, the most obvious examples of abstract objects are those of mathematics. Just as the Form of Beauty is distinct from beautiful things, so the number 2 is distinct from pairs of things that provide us with empirical representations of the number. A student who studies mathematics learns to perceive and manipulate the abstract entities that are numbers (algebra) and shapes (geometry). This puts them on a path that will enable them to perceive the most abstract of objects, the Forms, at least in Plato's view. That's why he thought philosophers first had to be proficient in mathematics among other disciplines. Only once potential philosophers were fluent with mathematical objects would they be prepared to perceive the Forms themselves.

Very few people today accept Plato's metaphysics, so that the rationale for barring young people from the study of philosophy no longer can be based in his ideas. Nonetheless, many philosophers agree with Plato that the very abstract nature of philosophy makes it an unsuitable subject for young people to study. This is the reason they would limit the study of philosophy to older students who had developed sufficient cognitive skills to engage in philosophical discourse.

As a result, philosophers have participated in the relegation of their own discipline to the fringes of pre-college education. Since philosophers do not believe that young students have the capabilities required for philosophical thinking, it's not surprising that there is such widespread reluctance to introduce philosophy into the curricula of elementary schools.

A growing number of philosophers and educators in the United States and, indeed, across the globe have rejected this idea and come to realize that young people deserve the opportunity to study philosophy. Given the prevalence of the opposing view—that young people are not capable of doing philosophy—it is imperative that there be a sustained and systematic justification for teaching philosophy to young people. This book provides that justification, something not needed in fields that are widely assumed to be necessary for the education of young people, such as mathematics.

The book you have before you is the third one I have written about doing philosophy with young children. *Big Ideas for Little Kids: Teaching Philosophy Through Children's Literature* is a how-to guide for those interested in introducing children to philosophy using picture books. *A Sneetch Is a Sneetch and Other Philosophical Discoveries: Finding Wisdom in Children's Literature* provides an introduction to philosophy for adults that uses picture books to present philosophical ideas and theories.

Thinking Through Stories has a different aim than my two earlier books. I write it as a p4/wc practitioner who has been facilitating philosophical discussion among children for a quarter of a century. During that time, I have become increasingly cognizant of the need to provide children with the opportunity to take part in philosophical discussions. I have learned about the variety of different approaches people have taken to this project and seen it in action around the globe. At the same time, I felt a need to justify the passion I have for this endeavor and to explain why I see picture books as an excellent way to introduce philosophy to elementary-school children that is also a good way for adults, be they teachers, parents, or just interested citizens, to begin facilitating such discussions.

1.2 Why Should We Teach Children Philosophy?

The two chapters that follow this one form the first section of the book and begin its argument in earnest by discussing why it is of critical importance to teach young children philosophy. Many people follow Plato in thinking of philosophy as a difficult subject that requires a great deal of maturity for its study. But the activity of philosophizing comes naturally to children as they attempt to understand their own experience. This is one of the reasons why it is important to give them the opportunity to take part in philosophical discussions.

Chapter 2 begins by looking at the traditional rationale for teaching children philosophy, namely that they lack the ability to reason. While this might explain *adults'* interest in having children learn philosophy, it doesn't explain why teaching them philosophy makes sense from a *child's* point of view. I present three justifications for introducing philosophy in elementary school that a child could endorse: engaging in philosophical dialogues *enhances* children's sense of self, *provides* a safe space for the discussion of issues that they are confronted with in living their lives, and *develops* an admirable method for resolving conflict that the children can use in other contexts.

Chapter 3 presents an additional and very important rationale for introducing children to philosophy that has not been as widely recognized as it should be: thinking philosophically supports children's innate sense of *wonder* about the world. Although young children's capacity for wonder is indicated by their repeatedly asking "Why?," as they grow older they routinely lose that capacity, partly as a result of adults' interest in suppressing their nearly constant questioning. But, like children, philosophers also have a heightened sense of wonder in comparison with your average adult. Thus, children's sense of wonder provides a significant reason to support their inclination to pursue the study of philosophy.

Another aim of this book is to demonstrate the validity of using picture books as what we call "prompts" or "stimuli" for philosophical dialogues. I begin to make my case for this position toward the end of Chapter 3, where I demonstrate that the appeal of Arnold Lobel's wonderful Frog and Toad story "Cookies" lies in the coincidence of: (i) the philosophical puzzles surrounding the concept of will power; (ii) children's development of the capacity to exercise will power or what psychologists call "executive function" between the ages of 3 and 5; and (iii) children's struggle to exercise that capacity in their lives. The conjunction of these three factors helps us understand why discussing "Cookies" can be so engaging and helpful to children, providing support for my advocacy for doing philosophy with young people using picture books.

1.3 Why Picture Books?

The second section of *Thinking Through Stories* focuses on different methodologies for introducing philosophy to young children. The two central methods that I consider use *stories* as prompts or stimuli for philosophical discussions. The question I pose is what are the advantages and disadvantages of using novels expressly written for philosophy discussions as opposed to commercially published picture books and other forms of children's literature.

Chapter 4 considers the use of novels expressly written for philosophy discussions. Although such novels have many advantages, such as expressly foregrounding the philosophical issues they focus upon, I use one chapter from Matthew Lipman's *Harry Stottlemeier's Discovery* to illustrate a problem with them. My argument is that the desire of the authors of such books to present a philosophical issue to children can lead to the use of theories that don't match the narratives of the books. This argument functions as a warning about using such texts to initiate philosophical discussions.

The fifth chapter of this book takes up a challenge that has often been made to those of us who use picture books in our discussions with children: it is inappropriate to have illustrations in the books used for elementary-school philosophy lessons. Since one aim of this book is to champion the use of commercially produced picture books—books that are notable for the manner in which they meld text and images—I show that this criticism is based upon a misunderstanding of the role that the illustrations play in picture books. Using the example of Maurice Sendak's classic *Where the Wild Things Are,* I show that the images in a picture book are not simply there to provide illustrations of events described by the written text. Instead, we should acknowledge that the images have an independent role to play in furthering the narrative of such books. Once we do so, we can dispense with this criticism of them and recognize picture books as excellent stimuli for philosophical discussions among young children.

Chapter 6 tackles a more theoretical issue by arguing that some picture books actually *do philosophy*. This is a highly controversial claim. To justify it, I take a detailed look at another Frog and Toad story, "Dragons and Giants." The story focuses on bravery, with the two protagonists trying to determine whether or not they are brave, like the heroes of the fairy tales they have been reading. At issue is the question of whether brave people experience fear. I argue that the story presents a counter-example to the assertion, made by Toad early in the story, that brave people do *not* experience fear. As such, it is actually doing philosophy and thus models the type of reasoning that the children themselves are to engage in during their philosophy sessions.

1.4 Issues about Using Picture Books

The final section of this book addresses some issues that arise about the use of picture books as prompts for philosophical discussions. In each of the three chapters in this section, I try to allay fears about difficulties that could arise when using picture books in philosophical dialogues.

One issue that has divided practitioners of p4/wc is how much philosophy a facilitator needs to know in order to successfully oversee an elementary-school philosophy discussion. Although many p4/wc programs require people to take part in the training sessions, I argue in the seventh chapter that adults can successfully facilitate such dialogues without having taken part in formal training sessions. I point out that there are many resources available either on the World Wide Web or in written texts that can be used to help beginning facilitators acquire the necessary knowledge and skills for moderating a philosophical discussion. My aim is to reassure teachers, parents, and other adults that they can embark on the voyage of philosophical facilitation without having to undergo formal training in either philosophy or facilitation.

Can we use picture books to discuss "difficult topics" such as racism? Recently, practitioners of p4/wc have debated the viability of discussing such issues using picture books as stimuli. Chapter 7 defends picture books as being suitable for such discussions at the same time that it acknowledges that certain picture books that have been recommended for such purposes are not suitable. The issue is whether some picture books present so reductive a view of complex phenomena like racism that they actually hinder young people from developing an adequate understanding of them. I show that, to the contrary, there are some picture books that do justice to the social and historical complexities of such phenomena, making them suitable for initiating a discussion of these issues in an elementary-school classroom.

One type of books that presents real challenges to facilitators are those containing stories with morals. Fairy tales are one example. They often end with a moral, such as "A stitch in time saves nine." The presence of such definitive morals makes it hard to envision a philosophical discussion evolving that questions the assumptions made by these stories. In Chapter 9, I show that there are various techniques that can be used to foster a genuine investigation of the ideas presented by such moralistic stories, making them suitable stimuli for philosophical discussions.

I conclude the book with a brief and very schematic survey of some other methods for facilitating philosophy discussions. I explain their advantages even as I point out that a number of them require more background than my preferred method of using picture books.

As I look back over the years of my engagement with introducing young children to philosophy, I realize that, at the outset of my interest in this work, there was no suitable book that explained both the importance of introducing young children to philosophy and also why picture books were an excellent stimulus to use to begin the dialogues the children would engage in. I have written this book in the hope that it meets both these needs: it presents a number of arguments for the importance of introducing children to philosophy while also showing why picture books are a great way to get children to appreciate the joys of doing philosophy.

Note

1 Matthew Lipman, the founder of the philosophy for children movement, used the formula p4c as a handy way to refer to it. Later, critics argued that the philosophy was actually something that was produced *with* the children and used the formula pwc as more appropriate. I have simply combined the two in order to refer to the various different approaches for doing philosophy with young children.

PART I

The Case for Philosophy for/with Children

2
WHY TEACH CHILDREN PHILOSOPHY?

The standard rationale for doing philosophy with children is the one that Matthew Lipman gave for developing the first contemporary philosophy for children program. Lipman was a professor at Columbia University who came to believe that his university students did not know "how to think," that is, they were not aware of the canons of logical thought. Lipman also claimed it was too late to teach university students this fundamental skill, one they should have learned much earlier in their academic careers. For this reason, he left his tenured position and went to Montclair State College, now University, where he founded the Institute for the Advancement of Philosophy for Children (IAPC).

Unfortunately, reference to teaching children how to *think* does not provide a clear justification for teaching *philosophy* to children. For one thing, children do know how to think. They can make all sorts of inferences and do so many times each day. What does Lipman mean when he says that his college students didn't know how to think?

In addition, it is not clear why a desire to teach students how to think provides a sufficient justification for introducing them to philosophy? While it may be true that the ability to think is an important skill to have, it's not self-evident why this provides a rationale for introducing children to *philosophy* more generally, for philosophy is not solely concerned with thinking. Philosophy addresses many fundamental concerns that human beings face during the course of their lives. If one's central goal is to teach children how to think, it's not evident that philosophy fits the bill.

The standard move made by defenders of the thinking rationale for teaching philosophy to children links that practice to the ideas of the pragmatist

DOI: 10.4324/9781003257455-3

philosopher, John Dewey. Essentially, Dewey treats the ability to think as a necessity for a democratic citizenry. He believed that, to participate in a democratic society, citizens need to be able to assess information critically and independently so as to be able to make up their minds in a reasonable manner. Since logic includes the study of informal fallacies or the fallacious inferences that people use in their daily lives, studying logic enables students to assess, for example, claims that politicians make, helping them discern when a politician has made a logical blunder. The argument is that exposure to philosophy helps children acquire the necessary skills to be effective citizens of a democracy, who can think for themselves.

Especially in the current political climate, in which terms like "fake news" and "witch hunt" circulate widely and frequently, it is important for citizens to have the ability to assess the truth of any statement put forward by an expert or a politician. One benefit of introducing young students to the canons of rational argumentation—something central to philosophy—is that it gives them the tools necessary to assess the validity of claims they hear or read, including everything coming from politicians and through the news media.

So, introducing students to the canons of logical thought provides a coherent rationale for their studying philosophy. Still, this doesn't explain why students should be introduced to many of the specific topics that have puzzled philosophers over the centuries. Would thinking about the relationship between the mind and the body, one of philosophy's "old chestnuts," really help a child be a democratic citizen? Discussing ethical issues like whether justice demands that society redress wrongs that it has committed will certainly help a child understand some of the important political issues of the day, but we need to understand how acquaintance with such issues will make them more independent and critical citizens, if this rationale is to stand as the grounds for introducing philosophy into elementary-school curricula.

2.1 There Are No Wrong Answers in Philosophy

I will begin to provide a more comprehensive defense of teaching philosophy to young children by telling you about an experience I had. When my son Jake was in elementary school, I attended many of the parent-teacher events at his school, the Jackson Street Elementary School, because I had been working there to help teachers introduce philosophy into their classrooms. At one such event, I arrived early and entered the empty classroom only to discover a former student waiting there. He was Asmir, the oldest son of a refugee family from Bosnia who emigrated during the Yugoslav civil war. He and his family had come to Northampton, Massachusetts, to evade the ethnic cleansing and sweeping of their native land.

Besnik smiled at me and said, "I remember you. You taught us philosophy."

"That's right," I replied. "How's middle school?" I asked him, for he had just begun sixth grade.

"They don't have any philosophy," was his response.

"Do you miss it?" I asked him.

"Yes," he said wistfully. "There are no wrong answers in philosophy."

Many philosophers who work with children, myself included, bristle at the claim that Asmir made: there are no wrong answers in philosophy. After all, when philosophers propose a theory, the response from other philosophers is normally a set of criticisms aimed at showing problems with the proposed theory. But teachers who are exposed to the idea of bringing philosophy into their elementary-school classrooms seem to inevitably drift to espousing the idea that philosophy has no wrong answers. We need to understand why this happens.

One possibility is that it reflects the novelty of our procedure for teaching philosophy. When working with elementary-school children, we aim to get them to participate in a genuine *dialogue* about a significant philosophical issue. In these dialogues, the facilitator will often not know the proper answer to the question being discussed (assuming that there is one!) or even the views philosophers have previously expounded on the topic. This is not what happens when they teach other subjects. A teacher who is teaching spelling knows the right way to spell a word and attempts to get their students to acquire this knowledge. But that is not how our philosophical dialogues proceed. We do not attempt to transmit philosophical knowledge to the students or to get them to embrace a particular philosophical position, such as, say, materialism, that is, the thesis that there is nothing in the world other than physical bodies. We don't even introduce them to any specialized philosophical terminology.

When we conduct philosophy dialogues among young children, our aim is for them to *articulate* their own beliefs about a complex philosophical issue, such as the nature of bravery, the subject of Arnold Lobel's philosophical classic "Dragons and Giants," a story I will return to in Chapter 6. We also help the children learn to support their own position with *reasons* and develop rational *criticisms* of the views put forward by other children even as they *respect* the contributions made by those they disagree with.

The person who is facilitating such dialogues acts much like an umpire in a sporting match. An umpire or referee does not take part in the game itself, but only watches to make sure that the rules are being followed and intervenes when they are not. In Chapter 7, I will spell out the rules for conducting a philosophical dialogue; for now, the point I wish to make is that, while playing this umpiring role, the facilitator abstains from making a substantive contribution to the conversation.

You'll recall that I was trying to understand why there is such a strong tendency among elementary-school teachers and their students to say, "There are no wrong answers in philosophy." Because the aim of a philosophical dialogue is not to teach students the right answer to a question, it's not hard to see why they might come to believe that standards of right and wrong do not apply to philosophy.

As I said, most philosophers, myself included, are critical of this claim. There are definitely wrong answers in philosophy and their wrongness is exposed by the withering critiques put forward by other philosophers. For example, the father of modern Western philosophy, René Descartes, argued in his *Meditations on First Philosophy* that the mind and body are two distinct substances that interact at a particular place in the brain, the pineal gland. Almost immediately, philosophers like Princess Elisabeth of Bohemia and Baruch Spinoza argued that interaction between different types of substances was incoherent. Substances can only interact with others of the same type. For this reason, Elisabeth and Spinoza argued that Descartes' dualistic metaphysics was deeply flawed and needed to be rejected.[1]

I've come to adopt a counter-slogan that captures my own sense of the issue concerning wrong answers and philosophy: "There may be no *right* answers in philosophy, but there are plenty of *wrong* ones!" The idea is that every theory a philosopher might propose will be flawed in one way or another, so that no theory can be taken to be the ultimate truth so sought after by philosophers. On the other hand, there are many theories that have been put forward by philosophers that have been rejected as mistaken, and that is as it should be. Just as we would be puzzled if a scientist said that he accepted the Ptolemaic universe with the earth at its center—a theory consigned to the dung heap by Galileo's astronomical observations—outmoded philosophical theories should also be rejected. For example, in attempting to save Cartesian dualism, Nicholas Malebranche argued that God insured that the mind and body would appear to interact even though they did not do so, a view adopted by Gottfied Wilhelm Leibniz through his idea of a preestablished harmony. Nowadays, no one would invoke God as the solution to metaphysical problems, so the views of these philosophers are now generally taken to be defective.[2]

This brings me back to Asmir. You'll recall that he told me that the reason he missed the opportunity to discuss philosophy in middle school was that there were no wrong answers. Rather than trying to explain to him why I thought there *were* wrong answers in philosophy, I began to reflect on why he experienced philosophy as having no wrong answers. I imagined this young refugee having to cope with the message that his answer to a question was wrong, his being told repeatedly, "No. You're wrong." This might have happened as a result of his not knowing English very well, at least at first. But it might also have been true in his other classes. And this would have led to his alienation from the whole idea of education as something that would make a difference in his life.

Although Asmir may have frequently had the experience of being told "You're wrong" in his elementary-school classes, when he took part in our philosophy classes that never happened. Instead, he blossomed when he could express his own ideas and found that his classmates appreciated what he had to say, valued his contributions to their discussions. I saw, or imagined, that I did, how *healing* the experience of taking part in a philosophy discussion was for him, someone whom I imagined having been beaten down by his previous experiences at school.

So, one answer to the question posed by the title of this chapter—Why teach philosophy to young children?—is that *it can enhance their sense of self.* Children rarely get asked by adults to tell them what they, the children, think about a topic. Yet that is precisely how our philosophy lessons proceed and this can be incredibly affirming to a young child.

When Julie Akeret, a local filmmaker, made a film about my the philosophy for children course I taught at Mount Holyoke College, she interviewed a mother of two children who attended the philosophy classes we offered for second graders at the Martin Luther King Jr. School. (I'll describe my course and our interventions at the school in more detail as I proceed.) "Both my kids loved it [the philosophy class]," she said. "They loved the idea that, as second graders, they were being asked questions and to give their opinions. That's very validating to a second grader … I think it gives them a sense of their worth and their ability. It makes them rise to the occasion."[3]

This parent's observations reflect the fact that our philosophy sessions generally began with the facilitator asking a philosophically significant question grounded in a picture book that had been read aloud to the children. Instead of seeing this as imposing the adult's agenda onto the children, this parent realized that an adult who asks the children a question can demonstrate their genuine interest in what children think about a topic. Being asked by an adult to explain what they think can be a significant positive experience for children, for it shows that the person asking the question respects their beliefs and is genuinely interested in what they have to say.

Incidentally, relying on the facilitator to begin the dialogue in Socratic fashion by asking a question contradicts one of the "idols" of p4/wc, that the teacher/facilitator should not begin the discussion. This is labeled "agenda setting" and it is anathema to many theorists of p4/wc beginning with Matthew Lipman. Because Lipman felt that school alienated children by not addressing issues that interested them, he wanted children to experience control of the discussion by setting the agenda themselves.

But we can see that there is a positive side to our practice of asking the first question that critics of it do not acknowledge: it lets children see that we are genuinely interested in *what they think*, something that they do not often encounter from grown-ups. This can be a very affirming and validating experience for a child, for they learn that their opinions matter and that they are deemed valuable by adults they admire. And once the conversation begins, the facilitator will not generally introduce new content into the discussion but only help the children follow the discussion where it leads, thereby giving the children control over the course the conversation takes.

2.2 Children as Natural-Born Philosophers

Philosophy began in Ancient Greece as an attempt to understand perplexing features of the world and the place of human beings in it. Although most contemporary adults no longer are in touch with these perplexing aspects of their lives, the Ancient Greeks were painfully aware of them as anyone acquainted with their literature will recognize. The great tragedies—from Aeschylus' *Orestia* to Sophocles' *Oedipus the King*—focus on deeply troubling aspects of human life by raising issues like: does a king's obligation to his followers outweigh his obligations to his family? And, does the knowledge available to human beings provide an adequate guide for determining how we should act? These are the sorts of issues Attic tragedies explored through the fates of their central characters.

The tragic fates that befell Agamemnon and Oedipus are an indication that the Greeks saw the world as a dangerous place that undermined human attempts to act morally on the basis of such knowledge as was available. This is the same context that spawned the first philosophers in the Western tradition. Since one of the central concerns of these pre-Socratic philosophers was understanding the perplexity they encountered when contemplating features of the world in which they found themselves, they developed theories to make that world less puzzling, more amenable to rational reflection. For example, the pre-Socratics worried about whether change was possible. They developed different accounts concerning the possibility of change. Heraclitus asserted the ubiquity of change, a view encapsulated in his famous saying that you can't step into the same river twice because new waters are always flowing. Parmenides, on the other hand, thought that reality was unchanging, static, so that our normal beliefs about change had to be consigned to the "way of non-being."

These questions fueled the speculations of the earliest Western philosophers and are quite similar to issues that perplex young children today. Lipman and his collaborator Ann Margaret Sharp agree, asserting that children "are much more akin to the pre-Socratic philosophers [than to the post-Aristotelian ones] whose aphorisms betrayed little awareness of philosophy (and its subcategories) as a unique, professional discipline" (Lipman and Sharp, 1986, p. 45). Because the pre-Socratics did not have a pre-existent canon of philosophy they could employ in their reflections, they were in much the same situation as young children, who have no previous acquaintance with philosophy as a discipline.

I recall when my 4-year old son asked me how the first human being came into existence. As he pointed out, I had two parents and each of them also had parents. He said that this was true of all human beings. What bothered him was the very first human, because its existence was paradoxical: if the first human being had parents, then it was not the first human being; if it didn't, then how could it have been born, come into existence?[4]

Jake's worry about the coming-into-being of the first human parallels concerns that animated the pre-Socratics. There is even a traditional philosophical problem—the Ship of Theseus—that bears witness to these concerns. Say that you have a raft and one of its boards is rotten. You replace it. Is the new raft the same raft as before the change? Most people say that it is since you have only replaced one plank. But what if another plank rots and is replaced? And then another? Is there a point when the raft is no longer the same raft? When would that be? And if not, how could still it be the same raft if all of its boards have been replaced so that there are no boards remaining from the original raft? Since change gives rise to paradoxes, Parmenides denied that reality could ever change, as I mentioned earlier. True being, he maintained, was eternal and unchanging, a view we have seen Plato adopt.[5]

My point here is that young children today continue to be puzzled by many of the same perplexing features of the world and their experience that triggered the reflections of the pre-Socratics and then their illustrious successors, Socrates, Plato, Aristotle, and the rest. For this reason, I view children as "natural-born philosophers."

The dominant educational practices in our society fail to recognize the natural, philosophical concerns that young children have. After all, it is quite unusual for philosophy to be taught in elementary schools, as I mentioned in the first chapter. Perhaps the impact of John Locke's metaphor of the mind as initially a "blank slate" retains its power, blinding many of us to the concerns that children themselves have. After all, if the mind at birth is nothing but a blank slate waiting to receive the sense impressions that will constitute experience, it seems that children cannot possibly already have their own questions about those experiences. As a result of its failure to include philosophy as a subject, our educational system may fail to meet one of the most important needs that children have, namely, that of finding meaning in their lives.

To choose another example, death is a topic that many educators may believe to be inappropriate to discuss in a public elementary school. Perhaps they think that the subject is simply too depressing to discuss with 6-year olds. But children naturally worry about death, as I pointed out I did as a young child. They may have had a relative who has died or heard about the killings that are unfortunately all too common on the streets of our cities and towns these days. And in the days of the pandemic, many of them may have unfortunately had a friend or relative who has died of COVID-19 and its complications.

So, a philosophical conversation—a dialogue—about death and what it means can be profoundly helpful to a child who is confronting the reality of death for the first time in their life. Rather than discussing this topic in the abstract, it can be helpful to use a picture book, such as *The Dead Bird* by Margaret Wise Brown (1938), to provide a means for discussing this difficult topic. In that book, a group of children find a dead bird and wonder about what happens to it after it has died. Once children encounter the idea that an animal's body will decay into constituents that become part of the natural world, being taken up by newly evolving entities in nature, they may not see death as scary as they initially did.[6] By providing them with a somewhat distanced means for thinking about the nature of death, a picture-book-based discussion can reduce the anxiety that the topic of death might ordinarily produce in children.

The topic of death also brings with it another reason why people may be reluctant to allow philosophy to be taught in schools. The topic of what happens to us after we die is one that is addressed by all religions and, at least in the United States, public schools are not supposed to address religious issues. Since most people don't draw a sharp distinction between philosophy and religion—after all, the two do share a concern for topics like death and the afterlife—it's not surprising that they would take the prohibition of religion from schools to apply to philosophy as well.

It is important to realize that philosophical discussions do not aim to produce conviction in the way that religious ones might. Although a philosophical discussion of death might include the question of whether something about us survives our deaths, it would not attempt to convince the children that there is a right answer to this question. (In that sense, there is no "right" answer to this question in a philosophy discussion.) Rather, the children will be encouraged to express their own views and to explain the reasons they have for their beliefs.

Death is certainly a topic that philosophers have pondered. Plato's earliest dialogues depict Socrates as he faces the prospect of his own death as a result of his being prosecuted for failing to respect the gods. At one point, Socrates even describes philosophy as a preparation for death. In the twentieth century, Heidegger saw virtually all of Western culture as an attempt to avoid thinking about death. There is no question that this topic is one about which philosophers have had a great deal to say.

Lest it seem as if philosophy only deals with depressing topics—a view I recall my mother having as she worried about what my life would be like as a professional philosopher—I should emphasize the existence of many less anxiety-producing topics about which young people are also puzzled. We have seen the question of identity through change as one of them. But they are also concerned, for example, with questions of justice and fairness, as they realize that being good is not always rewarded.

The conception of philosophy I have been describing does not begin with its formal procedures, such as the use of logic in valid argumentation. Instead, it focuses on how the *perplexity* induced by the troubling features of human life gives rise to the attempt to understand them and, hence, to the degree possible, control them. This is a specific, substantive conception to philosophy, one that naturally leads to the idea that even young children are a suitable audience for philosophy because, as we have seen, they are troubled by these very issues.

Introducing philosophy into the curriculum of elementary schools, then, is a way to bring *children's actual concerns* into the classroom. Because children generally find themselves puzzled by features of the world that are also the source of standard philosophical problems, they welcome the opportunity to discuss such issues with their classmates. When they do so, they are engaged in the same practice as professional philosophers, even though they have no knowledge of the history of the discipline or its overall structure.

I have been arguing that it is important to introduce philosophy into elementary-school classrooms. The questions with which philosophy is concerned, such as the nature of death or whether change is possible, have no clear, agreed-upon right answers. It might seem as if these questions cannot easily be addressed in the curricula of elementary schools. But these issues are existential ones that children naturally find themselves puzzled by in the course of living their lives and these issues continue to concern them once they have stumbled upon them. It is important that they have an opportunity to discuss their concerns and a classroom that incorporates philosophy gives the children the opportunity to do just that. As a result, they become more comfortable with questions that don't have clear-cut answers.

2.3 Philosophy as a Form of Conflict Resolution

There is another aspect of what children get out of philosophy discussions and that is a method of peaceful and respectful conflict resolution. I hadn't realized this benefit of doing philosophy until a teacher called it to my attention. She talked about witnessing a disagreement among children on the playground. After a conflict broke out among children playing a game, some of them said, "We've been doing philosophy. We know how to handle disagreements."

Here is how Lisa Hall, a teacher at the Martin Luther King School in Springfield, MA, described what she witnessed one day: "I remember a time when we were on the playground… The children got into somewhat of an altercation. I saw them all huddled together and came to find out there was a conflict between a couple of students … What I saw was they were implementing some of the philosophy techniques they learned … They remembered if you want to resolve any conflict, you first have to listen. Let each person speak, get all that they want to say out, and then go to the next person. The conflict was squashed, the children went on to play their game, and everyone was happy."[7]

Although initially I was pleasantly surprised by Ms. Hall's remarks about the children applying what they learned during our philosophy lessons to a conflict occurring on the playground, I came to see how appropriate it was. One way to think about what the students learn during philosophical dialogues, aside from articulating answers to the philosophical issues they have discussed, is precisely how to work toward resolving a conflict in a peaceful manner that respects all of the participants. When children express their opinions about a contested philosophical topic—such as whether it is morally permissible to tell a white lie to a dying person—it is likely that the children will disagree about it. As Ms. Hall says, in order to even attempt to resolve the disagreement, you first have to listen to what each person has to say, acknowledging that everyone has something useful to contribute to the discussion. When there is a disagreement, it's very important for all the parties to the dispute to feel that the group has heard their point of view. This helps them move toward a solution, for the emotional rancor that can fuel a disagreement gets dissipated when the participants in the dispute get time to have their say. In this context, it is important to emphasize that philosophy discussions do not necessarily seek to produce consensus among the participants, but only to clarify what the reasons for their disagreement are.

Of course, listening to the participants is just one aspect of a philosophy discussion and, in this case, a non-philosophical dispute resolution. During a philosophical conversation, the participants have to assess the validity of the claims they have heard by considering whether the reasons advanced in support of a position are compelling. This attitude can be transferred to the playground, as the children did, by considering the validity of what each of the participants in a dispute says. Coming to a peaceful and respectful resolution of a dispute is a regulative ideal of philosophical dialogues and also, as we have just seen, of playground etiquette.

This is a good time to mention the importance of conceptualizing the discussions in a philosophy for/with children class through the term *dialogue*, the term that Plato adopted to characterize his own method of doing philosophy. A dialogue is a discussion among two or more participants that aims at answering a question or resolving a dispute. Philosophy's origin in dialogues can be obscured by the fact that few written works take this form. But Socrates, who never wrote a word, took philosophy to be practiced through face-to-face interactions that attempted to answer such questions as "What is the nature of justice?"

Our own efforts with children are continuous with the practices of the Ancient Greeks that characterized the origins of Western philosophy.[8] Like Socrates, we take elementary-school philosophy to be realized in face-to-face dialogues among the school children who seek to resolve the philosophical issues raised by the picture books that have been read to them.

2.4 Conclusion

In this chapter, I have presented three reasons that children can accept for introducing philosophy discussions into their elementary-school classrooms: it enhances children's sense of self; it provides them with the opportunity to discuss issues that concern them; and it teaches them a peaceful means of conflict resolution. There are certainly other reasons. In the next chapter, I turn to one of these: doing so engages and enhances children's capacity for wonder. As I will argue, having the capacity to wonder is one of the hallmarks of childhood, and is a precious capacity that can all too easily be lost during the processes of maturation.

Notes

1 There is another feature of philosophy that may make it seem as if there are no wrong answers in philosophy. Even when a theory like Cartesian dualism has been discredited, other philosophers will take it up. Noam Chomsky, for example, is an unabashed Cartesian dualist and argues that it is the theory that best explains why children are so adept at learning languages. Nonetheless, the fact remains that, at least at a specific moment in time, there are wrong answers in philosophy, theories that don't stand the test of surviving criticism.

2 Unlike in the natural sciences, philosophical theories can return even after they had seemed to be refuted. Chomsky's support for Cartesian dualism is just one example of this phenomenon.

3 The video can be accessed at https://video.nepm.org/video/wgby-documentaries-big-ideas-little-kids/.

4 It might appear that Jake was asking a scientific question that was resolved by Darwin's theory of evolution. While I agree with this to an extent, it is important to recognize that the basis of Jake's worry was the impossibility of our experiencing an infinite sequence. This is a philosophical question that still puzzles philosophers as well as ordinary people.

5 There have been many attempts to provide a solution to the Ship of Theseus problem. Aristotle distinguished two different criteria for identity, one based on the material composition of something—same material—and another based upon its structure—same form.

6 According to *National Geographic*, children begin to understand the finality of death at age 4. See Virginia Hughes, "When Do Kids Understand Death," accessed on December 19, 2020 at: https://www.nationalgeographic.com/science/phenomena/2013/07/26/when-do-kids-understand-death/

7 Ms. Hall makes this comment in the video referenced in footnote 3.

8 In his recent two-volume book *Corrupting Youth*, Peter Worley also uses Ancient Greek philosophy as a guide for understanding philosophy for children. His account, unlike mine, stresses the role of dialectic.

3

THE ROLE OF WONDER IN CHILDHOOD

"Wonder is the heaviest element in the periodic table of the heart.
Even a tiny piece of it can stop time."

–Diane Ackerman[1]

In this chapter, I put forward a reason for introducing young children to philosophy that has not received the attention it deserves. Its point of departure is a view of childhood as a distinct life stage with various prominent features. Most centrally, it focuses upon young children's enormous capacity for *wonder*. It is their ability to experience the world as a strange place that provokes astonishment and presents a need for explanation that allies children with the discipline of philosophy, thereby making the practice of teaching them philosophy not just a good idea but a truly essential one.

To highlight the uniqueness of this conception of childhood, I compare it to that developed by the highly influential psychologist, Jean Piaget. Many of Piaget's ideas have had a huge impact on educational theory and practice as well as on society's view of children. For this reason, it is important to be clear about their shortcomings, for he denies children's ability to philosophize.

Piaget sees childhood as fundamentally a stage during which children must prepare for adulthood. From this perspective, the child is deficient in many of the capabilities possessed by a mature, functional adult. A simple example is language. Children come into the world without the ability to speak. During childhood, they learn to do so in a natural way. In schools, this ability is refined as children learn writing and reading, and concomitant skill of spelling and mastering new vocabulary.

DOI: 10.4324/9781003257455-4

There are many similarities between children's acquisition of language and their encounter with philosophical issues. Both of these happen naturally, as children encounter the strange and fascinating world they inhabit. And just as a child's language learning provides an important element of their early education, the same should be true of philosophy. Children need to have the opportunity to discuss the philosophical problems they encounter with both their peers and sympathetic adults. This is one reason why introducing philosophy into elementary-school curricula is so crucial.

3.1 Piaget's "Deficit" Model of Childhood

Because of the enormous impact Piaget's views about children and education have had on our thinking, it is important to understand both their insights and limitations. One of the most important early advocates for doing philosophy with children, Gareth B. Matthews, is highly critical of Piaget's view. He labels Piaget's understanding of childhood as a *deficit* model (Matthews, 2008). This is an important insight, so let's investigate exactly what it means.

On Piaget's view, the adult is normative. That is, the functioning adult is taken as the standard or norm to use in judging human beings at other stages of development. Adults generally have a variety of different skills, capacities, and abilities that together constitute their "adulthood." For example, adults are competent speakers of their native language. Although there are a very large number of human languages, most adult have mastery over their native language, which they learned to speak when they were children, and many are competent speakers of at least one other language. The capacities necessary to have mastery of a language include the ability to speak, read, write, and spell, as well as to understand utterances made in the language.

Linguistic ability is only one of a myriad of skills adult humans possess. Generally speaking, they are able to walk upright, hold various tools and utensils, control different machines, throw balls, etc. According to the Harvard Center on the Developing Child, the following are the five "underlying core capabilities" that adults possess: planning, focus, self-control, awareness, and flexibility.[2] These form the fundamental capacities that specify what is necessary to be a fully functional adult.

Children generally lack all of these capabilities. They tend not to plan very well because they are impulsive and won't follow plans that do not accord with their momentary desires. Nor do they exhibit the capacity to focus, as they are easily distracted causing their attention to wander. Self-control is certainly something that we want children to learn as they develop, but young children have difficulty not giving in to their immediate desires and exhibit some stunning lack of self-control. (We'll discuss this more in the context of "Cookies," a Frog and Toad story, later in this chapter.) It's not clear what "awareness" refers to, but if it is taken to amount to self-consciousness, then children lack that as well, for they tend to be so absorbed in whatever task they are perform-ing that they lack the self-conscious awareness typical of adults, who generally have the ability to become aware of the fact that they are engaging in a task. Finally, we can question whether children are flexible, but anyone who has tried to get their child to taste new foods will testify that children tend to be more rigid than adults, at least in regard to certain things.

Given the centrality of these five capabilities to adult life, it's easy to envi-sion their attainment as the goal of child development. Since a child has a deficit in regard to each of these capabilities, they ideally need to acquire them during the maturation process into adulthood they undergo. Although they have the potential to become full-blooded adults, they require appropriate training in order to achieve this goal. Children are different than the young of other animal species that rely much more on instinct and require less explicit training.

Once one accepts this idea of children as deficient adults, the goal of edu-cation emerges naturally. Education needs to support the development in chil-dren of the adult capabilities they lack. Doing so will remove the deficits that children are burdened by and allow them to become fully functioning adults. This forms the first element in Piaget's conception of childhood.

There is another very important aspect to Piaget's conception of childhood. It seems obvious that it is not possible to "fill up" all of a child's deficits at once. The transformation of a child into an adult is a process that takes time. To conceptualize this process, Piaget proposed that children's maturation takes place through a series of *developmental stages*, each of which has a characteristic "task" that a child must master.

The first stage, according to Piaget, is *the sensory-motor stage* that children inhabit from birth until the age of 2. Infants have to master their ability to control their own bodies, and this is the main task for this developmental stage. Very young infants have to learn that they can move their hands and feet. They do have certain innate capacities, such as being able to suck. But there is a lot they need to learn about their ability to control their bodies and interact with their environment.

The pre-operational stage occurs from ages 2 to 7. During this time, according to Piaget, children are egoists. This has important consequences for philoso-phy for children since this is generally the time when children are first intro-duced to philosophy in p4/wc programs. According to Piaget, at this stage the focus is on important capabilities that children lack. First, he thinks that they lack the ability to empathize with others. Since empathy, arguably, underlies ethical thinking—it is argued that one has to be able to empathize with others in order to consider their point of view—children at the age of 7 and below are not capable of ethical reasoning, according to Piaget. Piaget also holds a related view, namely that young children at this stage are concrete thinkers, so they are not able to discuss abstract issues. As we shall see, the practice of discussing philosophy with children demonstrates the falsity of both of these Piagetian claims.

From the age of 7 to 11, children are in *the concrete operational stage*. At this point in their development, children are beginning to learn how to reason, but they do so only from concrete starting points. They are not yet capable of genuine abstract thought. From the viewpoint of philosophy for children, this is a serious charge, for philosophy requires the ability to think abstractly.

Finally, the child of age 12 enters into *the formal operational stage*. This is the first time that a child is able to consider hypothetical situations according to Piaget. Only when they have reached this stage are children able to consider "what if...?", the sort of hypothetical situation that philosophers often rely on. Once again, this seems to entail that children younger than 12 lack the ability to think philosophically, for they are not yet able to think abstractly.

The impact of Piaget's stage theory helps explain the absence of philosophy from elementary-school curricula. If children are as deficient in the ability to reason abstractly as Piaget thought, they would simply be incapable of taking part in philosophical dialogues, for these require the ability to think hypothetically.

As my comments have already indicated, philosophers who have worked with children are critical of Piaget for failing to acknowledge children's ability to take part in philosophical discussions. Although children do dwell in the concrete much of the time, even at a young age they are capable of the abstract thinking required for doing philosophy. The sort of developmental model proposed by Piaget cannot do justice to children's philosophical abilities.

Lipman and Matthews, two of the first practitioners of and advocates for p4/wc, were both critical of Piaget's account. Lipman characteristically focuses upon reasoning and notes that adults are not eager to learn the principles of legitimate inference, although children are. But this means that children are not the ones lacking a capacity in this regard, adults are. As a result, Lipman challenges Piaget's contention that, as they get older, children naturally develop the capacities necessary for living a full life.

> Indeed, this must be one of the most paradoxical characteristics of our culture, the acquisition by adults of an incapacity not generally found in children. The indisposition of adults to learn reasoning contrasts so sharply with the readiness of children to learn it (along with language) that we must face the fact that *getting older is in some respects not growth but diminishment.*
>
> (*Lipman et al., 1980, p. 5, emphasis added*)

Lipman's claim that aging involves the diminishment of certain capacities undercuts the Piagetian model of children as deficient adults. In certain respects, children have capacities that adults lack, so that we cannot view aging as simply a process in which children acquire a set of capacities that they lack but adults possess. It is also a process that includes significant loss.

Matthews also points out that children are better at certain things than adults are. Like Lipman, he points to language learning as something children do much better than adults. But he also discusses the creation of works of art. He asserts that children have "gifts as artists that will likely not persist through adolescence into adulthood" (Matthews, 2008, p. 28). Finally, he points to children's interest in and ability to do philosophy as further evidence that children have abilities that adults lack, and he argues we should jettison the deficit model of childhood in favor of what he terms "the mirror-image conception of childhood" (Matthews, 2008, p. 40) that acknowledges that children share certain capacities with adults and are better at some things than adults, while also acknowledging that they lack certain abilities that adults have.[3]

All of this suggests that Piaget's understanding of children and their capacities is flawed. A different view of the child is needed, one that acknowledges their capacities as well as deficiencies. Is it possible that consideration of the philosophical interests and abilities of young children might provide a more suitable way to think about childhood than that advocated by Piaget and those he has influenced?

It is not only philosophers who have been critical of Piaget's views. Recently, developmental and cognitive psychologists have radically revised Piaget's conception of childhood. They have argued that even very young children have many more capacities than Piaget recognized. For example, as we have seen, Piaget claimed that children under the age of 12 are not able to consider hypothetical situations, that is, situations that are imagined alternatives to the real world. But even young babies, it is now known, are able to think about imagined situations. In fact, their lives are devoted to, among other things, creating a causal theory of the world and this requires them to think about counterfactual or hypothetical situations.

In an excellent summary of recent research on babies, Alison Gopnik (2009) proposes a different understanding of the differences between babies and adults than Piaget's. She points out that babies are much more interested in *play* than adults, who tend to focus on *achievement*, getting things done. But babies play is anything but frivolous, she points out. Through play, babies develop an understanding of both the external world and the psychological inner world of people.

So, the verdict of both philosophers and psychologists is that the deficit model is inadequate and needs to be replaced with an account of childhood that acknowledges all of the varied skills that children and even babies are developing as they face the world for the first time. This suggests that we would do well to acknowledge how creatively children respond to all of the stimuli that they are confronting for the first time.

3.2 Childhood and Wonder

One of the most frustrating features of young children, at least for their care-takers, is their incessant asking "Why?" No matter what you are doing—going on a shopping trip, heading to school, rushing to make a train—children are susceptible to distraction. They notice things that they find puzzling and then proceed to ask "Why?" For adults, who are focused on achieving their own aims, such questioning is often distracting, something they choose to stifle as they proceed on their shopping trip or whatever task they are currently engaged in performing. Unlike children, the achievement orientation of adults gets in the way of their taking children's questions seriously.

What makes children such obsessive questioners? The answer is that they are constantly confronted by phenomena they have never seen before and which do not make sense to them. They might, for example, look up at the sky and wonder not just why it is blue—the stereotypical child's question—but where it is. Sure, it's above us, but is there a big dome that is painted blue some 50–100 miles above our heads? The cosmology of the Greeks reflected something like this view, for they thought that there was a great sphere over our heads. It was this that they believed constituted the sky.

Unlike adults, children find the most basic features of the world to be extremely puzzling, in part because of its novelty. If we operate with the deficit model of childhood, it would seem that children's incessant questioning is the result of their lack of understanding, something that will decrease as they acquire knowledge about the way things work.

However, from the point of view of practitioners of philosophy for children, children's need to question and adult's imperviousness to their questions needs to be conceptualized differently. As we saw Lipman claim, there are ways in which children *lose* something as they age, the very "something" that fuels their desire to know "Why?"

The central characteristic of children that accounts for them asking so many questions is their susceptibility to *wonder*. When they encounter something novel that puzzles them, they wonder about it: what exactly is it? what does it do? why is it there? will it always be like that? These are some of the questions a new phenomenon can give rise to in children, always sparked by their sense of wonder.

Adults generally do not share the ubiquitous wondering so characteristic of children. As Lipman and his co-authors say, "Many adults have ceased to wonder because they feel that there is no time for wondering, or because they have come to the conclusion that it is simply unprofitable and unproductive to engage in reflection about things that cannot be changed anyhow" (Lipman et al., 1980, p. 31). As a result, children absorb the adults' "prohibition against wondering" and acquire an attitude of passive acceptance of the mysteries of the world and human existence.

But what exactly is wonder? A good place to begin is with a dictionary definition, though we will see that it does not provide an adequate understanding of the term. Among the definitions of wonder given by the *Oxford Dictionary of the English Language* (hereafter *OED*) is this one: "The emotion excited by the perception of something novel and unexpected, or inexplicable" (p. 3809). Let's examine it carefully to see the extent to which it illuminates the nature of wonder.

The first thing to note about this definition is that it classifies wonder as an emotion. Emotions are themselves complex states of mind, having at least a feeling and a cognitive component. When the *OED* states in the first clause of its definition that wonder is *caused* by "something novel and unexpected, or inexplicable," it is characterizing the *cognitive* component of wonder, the conceptual content that is part of the emotion. The claim is that wonder is caused by a person's witnessing something that they take to be new and unusual.

While being a response to something new and unusual might be a sufficient criterion for wonder, it certainly is not necessary. The philosopher Immanuel Kant claimed that "Two things fill the mind with ever new and increasing wonder (*Bewunderung*) and awe, the more often and steadily we reflect upon them: the starry heavens above me and the moral law within me" (*Critique of Practical Reason*, V: p. 151–152). Since neither the starry heavens nor the moral law is novel or unexpected, an adequate characterization of the cognitive component to wonder would have to be amended to include these phenomena as capable of producing the state of wonder.

The second clause of the *OED*'s definition focuses upon the feeling component of wonder. Astonishment, perplexity, bewilderment, and curiosity are all feelings that we have. The definition claims that, when we have such feelings *and* they are caused by something that is unexpected and novel, then the emotion we are experiencing is wonder. But these feelings are not all equivalent. When we watch a magician perform a trick, we may be astonished that they were able to, say, read a person's mind. While we might be curious about how they did it, we don't necessarily have to be. And while we can be curious about how a COVID-19 vaccine was developed, we wouldn't necessarily be astonished that it was, even as we might marvel at the speed with which the development took place.

In his essay on "The History of Astronomy," Adam Smith distinguishes wonder from two of the other emotions with which he believes it is often confused.

> Wonder, Surprise, and Admiration, are words which, though often confounded, denote, in our language, sentiments that are indeed allied, but that are in some respects different also, and distinct from one another. What is new and singular, excites that sentiment which, in strict propriety, is called Wonder; what is unexpected, Surprise; and what is great or beautiful, Admiration.
>
> (*Smith, 1799, p. 1*)

Smith thinks that the emotions of wonder, surprise, and admiration are often confused with one another and so he attempts to distinguish them. Wonder, he says, has as its object something "new and singular." An astronomer who observes a new planet will experience wonder, according to Smith, but not surprise or admiration. Recently, a ring of six stars circling each other was discovered. One of the scientists describes the discovery as "blowing my mind."[4] That expression suggests surprise rather than wonder, calling into question Smith's claims.

Smith goes on to claim that, when something unexpected occurs, the emotion we feel is surprise. If I'm driving home and, as I turn a curve, see a car stopped in the middle of my lane, I will be surprised, for it is not something that I expected to see. I might wonder why the car is stopped there, so that the two emotions can occur together in response to the same event. (Of course, there will be other emotions also present, such as anxiety that I may not be able to stop my car in time to avoid a crash.)

Finally, admiration is the emotion caused by something great or beautiful, according to Smith. Looking at a great painting, such as Picasso's *Les Demoiselles d'Avignon*, according to Smith, can give rise to our admiration, but not our wonder or surprise. That seems odd to me. I can admire Picasso's painting while also wondering how he was able to create it, how he got, for example, the idea of including African masks in a representational painting of a group of prostitutes. While Smith is right to distinguish between these different emotions, his account of what causes us to experience each seems inadequate.

Focusing on art as a source of wonder in adults indicates that wonder is not an emotion that only children feel. Jesse Prinz has argued that theorists have had this mistaken view. "Wonder is sometimes said to be a childish emotion," he says, "one that we grow out of. But that is surely wrong. As adults, we might experience it when gaping at grand vistas" (Prinz, 2013). Prinz's claim mirrors Kant's, for Kant clearly experienced the emotion of wonder in regard to the heavens and the moral law.

Prinz goes on to acknowledge art as one area in which adults do experience wonder. In so doing, he suggests that there is another component to wonder, what he terms a *spiritual* one (Prinz, 2013). He connects this component to our interest in art, for when looking at great works, we often feel wonder and he believes that this wonder is not completely characterizable through the emotional and cognitive components just described.

Is there a spiritual component to wonder, as Prinz claims? Perhaps the idea is that, when we wonder at certain phenomena such as our view of the world from a mountain peak, our emotion does not accord with the standard view concerning wonder. One might not experience "astonishment mingled with perplexity or bewildered curiosity" when looking at the world from this vantage point, yet one could still feel wonder at the very existence of such an amazing spectacle. Characterizing wonder as having a spiritual component gives us a way of understanding this experience.

But is our experience of wonder as adults as limited as Prinz suggests? I think not. The crucial point is that adults are *achievement oriented*, a claim we saw Gopnik make in her attempt to distinguish the basic orientation of children from that of adults. Adults have various projects that they have undertaken in their lives and they are committed to completing them. This means that they do not want to be distracted by having to wonder about such impractical questions as where the sky is located. If you are trying to get dinner prepared for your family, you don't want to shift perspectives in order to reflect on such abstruse questions.

But this does not mean that adults cannot experience wonder in contexts other than being out in nature or inside a museum. There are myriad features of the world and our experience of it that are mysterious and thus suitable for wondering about. Take the idea of mind-body interaction that we have seen was the *bête noire* of Descartes' philosophy. How my thinking about a thought can make my body do something is really quite mysterious. Although the adult immersed in chopping onions can't really afford to step back and puzzle over their ability to command their arm to move, there are circumstances in which adults do wonder about such mysterious aspects of their experience.

Generally, what is needed in order for one to open oneself up to the wondrous, mysterious nature of our existence is having the time, the leisure to do so. When I sip a glass of wine before eating dinner, I find myself moving out of my goal-oriented orientation into a more detached and reflective mood. In that mood, I open myself up to the various mysteries of my life and thus the experience of wonder. At such moments, I am in touch with what poets and psychologists call "my inner child," my ability to be amazed by all the ordinary features of my life, my experience, that are as wondrous as anything produced by an artist.[5]

There is one more complication to our account of wonder, once more due to Smith. He points at the physiological changes that accompany the feeling of wonder when we attempt to understand something that we have not experienced before:

> It is this fluctuation and vain recollection [in regard to things we have not previously encountered], together with the emotion or movement of the spirits that they excite, which constitute the sentiment properly called Wonder, and which occasion that *staring*, and sometimes that *rolling of the eyes*, that *suspension of the breath*, and that *swelling of the heart*, which we may all observe, both in ourselves and others, when wondering at some new object, and which are the natural symptoms of uncertain and undetermined thought.
>
> (*Ibid., 14–15, emphasis added*)

Smith here points out that there are a number of physiological changes that occur when we feel wonder about something. This adds another component to our account of wonder, for this emotion is registered by the physiological changes to a person's body that help us distinguish it from other emotional states that are similar to it.

One implication of the account of wonder I have just proposed is that it is an emotion that aims at its own supersession. What I mean by this is that, when we experience wonder, we are motivated to resolve it, to achieve the type of understanding of a phenomenon that makes one no longer wonder about it. A child who learns that the color of the sky is caused by the refraction of light rays will no longer be tempted to ask why the sky is blue, though they still may retain a certain amount of amazement about this explanation of the phenomenon.

I began this investigation into the nature of wonder because I claimed that wonder was an emotion that explained children's persistent questioning. Because the world was new to them, children constantly are confronted by phenomena they have not previously experienced. As we have seen, this is precisely one circumstance in which wonder is produced in human beings. Adults have more experience of the world and therefore are not as susceptible to wonder as young children are. Childhood is a life stage characterized by the frequent experience of wonder.

But how does this discussion of wonder help us develop an alternative model of childhood to Piaget's developmental model that we saw to be deficient? I have emphasized the importance of wonder in the life of children. Because they are encountering the world and everything in it for the first time, there are many things—both objects and events—that they have not seen or heard or felt or tasted before. Since we have seen that wonder is often prompted when one encounters something for the first time, the novelty of the phenomena a child encounters makes wonder a normal feature of their lives.

We have seen that the emotion of wonder is a complex one made up of a number of distinct components. Since we are most interested in children's relation to wonder, it is useful to emphasize two feeling components of the emotion: puzzlement and astonishment. Any actual experience of wonder will likely have both of these components present, though in different proportions depending on circumstances.

With children, I would venture to say that the predominant aspect of the wonder that they experience is usually the recognition that they lack an understanding of the things they encounter in the world. That is why children so often ask us, "Why?": they find themselves in a world whose most fundamental features puzzle them, giving rise to the emotion of wonder. The questions that they ask are an attempt to gain an understanding of those things and resolve their wonder.

But even as they wonder, say, how the first human came into being—an issue that reflects their puzzlement—they will also experience astonishment that human beings actually exist. Both of the central feeling components of wonder thus come into play in a child's wonder about their world.

3.3 Philosophy, Wonder, and Children

The belief that philosophy begins in a sense of wonder has a long history in Western philosophy beginning with the Ancient Greeks. In his dialogue, *Theatetus*, Plato has Socrates identify wonder as the source of philosophy: "I see, my dear Theatetus, that Theodorus had a true insight into your nature when he said that you were a philosopher, for wonder is the feeling of a philosopher, and philosophy begins in wonder" (155 c–d). Socrates here claims that the feeling of wonder lies at the base of philosophizing. The idea is that people are prompted to philosophize because they find a feature of the world or their experience puzzling, something they are wondering about.

Aristotle agrees with Plato about the importance of wonder for philosophy. He claims in the *Metaphysics* that wonder is what prompted humans to philosophize (982b12). And subsequent philosophers have agreed. G.W.F. Hegel, for example, made the following claim while discussing "the symbolic form of art" in his *Lectures on Aesthetics* (1826): "The sentiment of art like the religious sentiment, like scientific curiosity, is born of wonder; the man who wonders at nothing lives in a state of imbecility and stupidity." Although Hegel does not mention philosophy here, it is clear that he thinks that wonder plays a role in all creative activities, philosophy included.

Søren Kierkegaard also acknowledged the relationship between wonder and philosophy, writing in his *Journal* on November 15, 1841, "It is a positive starting point for philosophy when Aristotle says that philosophy begins with wonder, not as in our day with doubt." (The reference to doubt is to Descartes.) Perhaps surprisingly, Martin Heidegger devoted a lecture to wonder in 1937–1938 and connected it to the origin of thinking in the sense intended by Plato and Aristotle (Heidegger, 1937–1938). Finally, a philosopher working in a different tradition, Alfred North Whitehead, stated in *Modes of Thought*, "Philosophy begins in wonder. And at the end when philosophic thought has done its best the wonder remains." Whitehead's claim that philosophizing does not put an end to the wonder we experience is important to bear in mind and is a useful corrective to thinking that philosophy can resolve our wondering.

Other philosophers have been more interested in trying to understand the function that wonder serves. We have already investigated Adam Smith's discussion of wonder. In *The Passions of the Soul* (1649), Descartes puts forward an explanation of the function that wonder serves in our lives: to "learn and retain in our memory things of which we were previously ignorant" (AT XI 384,

CSM I 354). Descartes here uses the standard account of wonder as caused by things of which we had no previous experience to develop an account of the function of wonder, one that links it to memory.

Descartes claim that wonder helps us remember things that we didn't previously know can help explain why wonder is often associated with children. Because children do not have the wealth of experience that most adults do, they are more likely to be surprised by simple things that happen to them. If we accept Descartes' claim that the function of wonder is to help us remember things that we were previously ignorant about, then we can understand why children will be much more likely than adults to experience wonder in relation to many of the ordinary things they encounter for the first time, for they need to build up a store of memories in order to feel at home in the world. Wonder provides the basis for remembering one's experiences and thus coming to feel less surprised by them.

It is striking that there are two very different groups of people who are considered particularly vulnerable to wonder: children and philosophers. This might suggest that there is a connection between the activity of philosophizing and children, one is mediated by the role of wonder in each.

This is, indeed, the case. As I mentioned in the last chapter, I have long maintained that children are "natural-born" philosophers, meaning that children have an innate tendency toward philosophical thought. We can now see that their susceptibility to wonder helps explain why this is so. Because children encounter so many new things in the course of living, they are constantly experiencing the emotion of wonder. In so far as they then wonder about the nature of the world and their experiences, they quite naturally fall into philosophical speculation, wondering about both mundane things—why is the sky blue?—and esoteric ones—is there a meaning to life? Once one recognizes the importance of wonder in the lives of children and its role in grounding philosophy, children's natural interest in philosophy becomes explicable.

Children's natural interest in philosophical questions makes it all the more important to introduce philosophy into their educations from an early age. We ought to be supporting their inquisitiveness in full awareness that the natural tendency will be for it to diminish as they become more experienced and find the world less startling than it initially appeared.

The complacency of most adults only makes it all the more urgent for our society to encourage children to keep wondering about the world and asking questions arising from their puzzlement. Like children, philosophers have managed to keep their sense of wonder alive as they ponder many of the perplexing features of the world and human experience.

Philosophically speaking, when one experiences the world as unintelligible, as containing many things that one does not understand, the result can be a feeling of alienation, of not feeling at home in the world. Although sometimes the sense of wonder can be a powerfully good feeling to have, as when, for example, I feel awe while listening to the third, slow movement of Beethoven's *String Quartet Op. 132*, this is different from the effect when one experiences things as not making sense. In the latter case, one naturally has a desire to understand what one has experienced. When one has acquired an understanding, one returns to a sense of being at-home in the world.

A child's questioning is an attempt to recapture this feeling. They yearn to return to a state in which they feel "at one" with the world, to dismiss their experience of alienation.

Doing philosophy with young children is one way to help them attain the feeling of being at home in the world. Whereas traditional schooling presents children with materials that they are told they need to master in order to progress, philosophy for children meets children where they are, seeking to resolve some of the perplexities that they find themselves experiencing.

The understanding of childhood that I am here advocating emphasizes the centrality and significance of children's ubiquitous wonder at the world and themselves. Instead of treating children's constant questioning "Why?" as a source of irritation, I suggest that we see it as a resource that can be put to good use in the context of their education. Children's desire to understand that which they find puzzling and about which they wonder provides the motivation that we can rely upon in the classroom. All that we need to do is to begin where the children already are—at a place of wonder at some significant feature of the world—and we will have solved one of the central issues in contemporary education, viz. finding a way to motivate children to learn. Because children possess an already existing desire to understand those things that produce in them a feeling of wonder, they are already motivated to engage in an educational process that promises to focus on the problems that *they* have a desire to solve.

3.4 Picture Books

In discussing the possibility of having dialogues with children about death, I mentioned a picture book. This foreshadowed the claim for which I will now argue: picture books are a particularly good way to initiate philosophical dialogues among children.

I shall now give one example of why this is so. As background, recall that children are faced with many developmental challenges as they grow. An important one is achieving what psychologists term "executive function or control." The psychologist Alison Gopnik defines this as the "ability to suppress what we want to do now because of what we will want in the future" (Gopnik, 2009, p. 148). She points out that this is a capacity that children develop between the ages of 3 and 5.

Arnold Lobel's charming Frog and Toad story "Cookies" from *Frog and Toad Together* (1979) focuses on the difficulties involved in exercising executive control as well as the paradoxical nature of the concept. In the story, the focus is on "will power," the philosophical expression of the psychologists' notion of executive control. The story begins with Toad bringing a batch of delicious cookies to Frog's house. They begin eating some cookies immediately. They taste so good that they can't stop eating them, despite their attempts to have "just one last cookie." Frog realizes they will get sick to their stomachs if they keep eating the cookies. He says that they need *will power*. Toad is puzzled and asks Frog what will power is. "Trying hard *not* to do something that you really want to do," responds Frog.

Frog then engages in a number of different activities to restrain the two of them from eating more cookies, but each time Toad finds a way to thwart Frog's intentions. First, Frog puts the cookies in a box but Toad points out that they can open the box and eat the cookies. When Frog ties the box closed, Toad says that they can cut the string to get access to the cookies. Toad then mounts a ladder to put the cookies out of their reach but the ever-resourceful Toad points out that they can climb the ladder to get the cookies.

In desperation, Frog goes outside and leaves the cookies for the birds who swoop down and eat them, leaving the two amphibians cookie-less. Toad is bereft but Frog points out that at least they have a lot of will power. Toad's response is to tell Frog he can keep his will power, for he's going home to bake a cake.

If we think about the situation of young children who are just learning how to exercise executive control, we can see how "Cookies" represents their struggles in a kind, gentle, and humorous manner. Toad lacks executive control, for his actions are impervious to reason and determined by his strong immediate desire to eat delicious smelling cookies. Frog, on the other hand, has begun to master executive control, so that he is able to adopt a range of different strategies to keep Toad and himself from getting sick from eating too many cookies. The "battle" between these two characters is an externalization of the struggles we all have when faced with an overwhelming desire we know we should not satisfy.

At the same time, we need to acknowledge that there is a philosophical problem about will power. In an article about "Cookies," Jeanette Kennett and Michael Smith identify it as "the paradox of self-control" (Kennett and Smith, 1996).[6] We can see the problem if we look carefully at Frog's definition of will power. He said that will power was trying not to do something you really wanted to do. The philosophical issue is whether such a notion is even coherent. After all, if you *really* want to do something, then you just do it. If you don't want to do something, then you don't. There seems to be no place for something like will power in the analysis of our actions.

It is the convergence of a young child's perplexity about the possibility of exercising will power and a philosopher's potential skepticism about the coherence of the concept of will power that makes "Cookies" such a great story to use to stimulate philosophical dialogues. Young children get introduced to a substantive philosophical issue that is one they likely have been dealing with in their own lives as they attempt to exercise control over their own desires. It is the correlation between children's lived experience and an abstract philosophical issue that fuels their enthusiasm for discussing whether or not Frog and Toad have will power at the end of the story as Frog claims.

"Cookies" is a paradigmatic example of why picture books are such a good means for beginning philosophical dialogues among young children. Picture books present issues in a charming and enjoyable fashion that engages young people—as well as adults. Because picture books can develop concerns that children have in their own lives into entertaining narratives that raise philosophical questions, they deserve to be seen as one of the most appropriate ways to get children involved in philosophical dialogues.

3.5 Conclusion

In this chapter, I have argued that children's capacity for wonder makes them particularly adept at doing philosophy. A story like "Cookies" is particularly well-suited to function as a stimulus for a philosophical dialogue because it focuses on a particular psychological capacity that children are just learning to manage, self-control or will power. The coincidence of a philosophical issue—Is will power a real phenomenon?—with a developmental issue for children— They only come to exhibit what psychologists call "executive control" between the ages of 3 and 5—allows the story to both capture the interest of children and stimulate them to take part in a philosophical discussion about the concept.

The final step in my argument is the claim that engaging in philosophical dialogues *enhances* children's sense of wonder. In part, this is because it is very unlikely that one, fairly short dialogue among a group of elementary-school children will provide a completely satisfying account of will power. After taking part in such a dialogue, children will retain a sense of puzzlement about aspects of will power, thereby confirming Whitehead's claim that wonder remains after philosophy has been done. For example, there is usually a disagreement about whether a person—and the two amphibians count as persons in this story because of the literary devices of personification—can have will power even after the temptation has been removed. In order to begin to provide an answer to this question, more distinctions have to be made, such as that between the possession and exercise of will power.[7]

So, it seems reasonable to believe that children who engage with one another philosophically will see the value of their questioning and will experience the discussion as supporting the importance of their feeling of wonder. Rather than curtailing children's desire to ask "Why?," philosophy can be the means of keeping children naïve in the positive sense of continuing to be puzzled about many features of the world and their experience of it.

Notes

1 From the introduction to a reading of "The Consolation of Apricots" at the 2018 *The Universe in Verse*. Quoted by Maria Popova in *Brain Pickings* for December 27, 2020.

2 https://developingchild.harvard.edu/science/deep-dives/adult-capabilities/#:~:text= Mounting%20research%20from%20neuroscience%20and,control%2C%20awareness% 2C%20and%20flexibility. Accessed on December 24, 2020.

3 Unfortunately, Matthews does not expand on what he takes the "mirroring" conception of childhood to involve and I am not sure what he intended this concept to refer to.

4 Robin George Andrews, "Six Stars, Six Eclipses: 'The Fact that It Exists Blows My Mind'," https://www.nytimes.com/2021/01/23/science/six-stars-eclipses.html

5 Sara Goering prompted this line of thought by a comment on a talk I gave on this material at the Central Division Meetings of the American Philosophical Association on February 24, 2012.

6 It is worth pointing out that these two professional philosophers use "Cookies" as the basis of their own analysis of will power. Even very simple picture book stories can provoke complex philosophical theory building such as that engaged in by Kennett and Smith.

7 Kennett and Smith make this and other distinctions in their attempt to justify Frog's claim to have will power at the end of the story despite the absence of temptation.

PART II

Why Picture Books?

4

THE USES AND LIMITATIONS OF PHILOSOPHICAL NOVELS

In the previous two chapters, I established the importance of introducing philosophy to children in elementary-school classrooms. We now need to reflect upon what the right way to do this is. Although virtually anything can initiate a philosophy discussion—a good discussion can take place by emptying your pockets and simply asking what all objects you find there have in common—there is general consensus that stories, narratives, provide the best means for getting children interested in philosophical issues. The question, then, is what type(s) of story is the most appropriate to use in elementary-school classrooms.

There are two fundamental approaches to the use of stories that have been developed within p4/wc. The first, pioneered by Matthew Lipman, is using philosophical novels that have been explicitly designed to raise philosophical issues in the minds of young students. The second, first proposed by Gareth Matthews but one that I have developed in my own work over the past quarter of a century, uses commercially published children's books—picture books and also chapter books.

In this chapter, I will concentrate on the use of novels expressly designed for teaching philosophy to children. In the following one, I will discuss the use of published picture books. My aim is to uncover the benefits and pitfalls of different approaches to doing philosophy with children.

4.1 Setting the Agenda

In our attempts to involve children in philosophical discussions, there is widespread agreement that we do not want to impose our own agenda on the discussion that should be the prerogative of the children. That is one difference

DOI: 10.4324/9781003257455-6

between the standard conception of ethics education and the way in which children discuss ethical concerns in philosophy for children sessions.

When educators emphasize the need for schools to engage students in ethics education, what they generally have in mind is the attempt to inculcate ethical values in children. For example, children need to be taught that the work they hand in has to be their own, that it is a violation of accepted moral principles to present someone else's work as if it were your own. The norm prohibiting a student from presenting as their own work that they have not done themselves is usually presented to students simply as a rule they have to follow at school. The idea is that telling them what the appropriate norms are for homework will simply translate into their acceptance of this norm or value, their acknowledging of plagiarism as unethical.

As philosophers, we are interested in having children think about ethical issues in education. However, when we do so, we don't *tell* the students how they should behave or what they should think. Rather, the goal is to have the children reflect upon, express, and discuss *their own views* on the ethical issues that are raised. To continue with my previous example, if the goal is to get children to think about the ethical norm that they should only turn in work that they themselves have done, we might ask them if they think it is wrong to present work that someone else has done as if it were your own. First, you could start by asking them to give some examples of doing that, such as by cheating on a test by copying someone else's answers. Once the children have offered a good range of examples, the facilitator might ask them if they think doing those things is morally wrong, something that they should not do? The hope is that children will be able to present a rationale for this norm that they find compelling, although there is no guarantee that this is what will happen.

This hope is not chimerical. I have frequently discussed the issue of plagiarism with young children. They generally respond by saying that handing in someone else's work as if it were yours is not *fair*. They explain that a person who did that would be getting credit for something that they had not done, and that this isn't fair because students should be judged on the basis of their own efforts. In so doing, they introduce a higher level norm—fairness—from which the norm against plagiarism can be derived.

This is an example of how, in philosophy discussions, children reach conclusions based upon their interactions with their classmates rather than by absorbing norms that have been presented to them as valid. The fundamental assumption governing philosophy for children is that the children should determine the course that the discussion will take, and this means that adults should not impose an outcome on the children's own discussion. Only if the children take clear ownership of the discussion, it is thought, will the results be ones that the children endorse and remember. In addition, their motivation for taking part in the discussion is thought to depend on their seeing the outcome of the discussion as one that is determined by them and not the adults supervising their interactions.

Teachers often have a hard time refraining from summarizing the results of a discussion for their students. I recall a session that I led with children at a school whose principal came to see how p4/wc worked. When our session ended, she intervened and told the children what conclusions they had reached. Although I said nothing at the time, I was upset that the principal felt compelled to tell the children what they had learned. To do so is often to distort the richness of the dialogue that has taken place.

While the point I have just made may seem obvious, philosophy for children practitioners often fall prey to their desire to ensure a positive outcome to the discussions they facilitate. This can lead them to adopt strategies that amount to *agenda setting*, that is, setting up the goal for the discussion. When they do so, their facilitating will be more directive than it should be, taking leadership away from the children, where it belongs. In what follows, we will be careful to note when such tendencies impinge upon the views we discuss.

4.2 Philosophical Novels for Children

The Philosophy for Children movement can be said to have begun in 1971, the year that Matthew Lipman published his first philosophical novel for children, *Harry Stottelmeier's Discovery* (hereafter *Harry*).[1] Soon afterward, because of the success of his initial attempts to bring philosophy into schools, Lipman founded the Institute for the Advancement of Philosophy for Children (IAPC) at Montclair State University (then Montclair State College). Lipman's program has been very influential, bringing philosophy into classrooms worldwide.

Lipman believed that the best way to teach children philosophy was by using philosophical novels that were written expressly for this purpose. *Harry* was the first such novel that Lipman wrote and there were a series of others to follow, most of them coauthored with Ann Margaret Sharp, Lipman's collaborator at the IAPC. Each novel focuses on a particular field of philosophy—*Harry* covered logic—and together the novels constitute a philosophy curriculum for children. Other philosophers have followed Lipman's ideas and written their own philosophical stories and novels, though they don't all abide by his dictates.

Although I have never used Lipman's novels in my work with children, I do respect their achievement. What's particularly nice about these novels is the way in which philosophical ideas are embedded in them. Their stories, while not great literature, present philosophical problems by having them emerge during discussions engaged in by the novels' young protagonists, thereby mirroring the sorts of discussions Lipman hoped the school children would themselves engage in.

Because the novels are written in order to raise philosophical issues for children to discuss, the issues can be presented in a manner that makes it easy to see what they are. For example, in *Kio and Gus*, here is how the philosophical problem about the nature of time arises in Gus' thoughts:

I try counting the grains of sand on the fingernail of just one pinkie: one, two, three, four .... oh, they're just too small and there's too many of them! How long would it take to count all that are on the beach here?

What if everything's made of little grains of sand? Could they be counted, one by one? Like in the hourglass that we have in the kitchen at home—one grain at a time?

One grain at a time. Each grain of sand takes up space. But if you take them one grain at a time, is that time?

See, that's why I like sand so much: when I think about it, my thoughts go in all directions!

If nothing moved, there'd be no time. But there is time. So it must be because things move.

Does that mean time is what happens when things move?

Or is time what we get when we measure how fast things move? Wow, my head is swimming![2]

Gus here raises a significant philosophical problem: what is time? As St. Augustine noted, this is a thorny problem: "What is time then? If nobody asks me, I know; but if I were desirous to explain it to one that should ask me, plainly I do not know" (St. Augustine, 2006, p. 242). Clearly, Gus is as puzzled as Augustine about the nature of time.

Anyone reading Gus' ruminations will realize that figuring out the nature of time is a serious philosophical problem. Because the novel raises this question directly, there is no need for textual interpretation to bring the problem into the consciousness of the children. The text itself raises the issue straight-forwardly, so that children can see that it is a problem that they might want to think about. When they do, they mirror Gus' philosophical musings.

Lipman also helps teachers use his novels by providing instructional manuals that they can refer to. These manuals highlight the philosophical issues that are presented in the text and provide teachers with a great deal of information and advice that can be useful to them when they teach these materials. In addition, Lipman also offered training sessions through the IAPC where people could learn the techniques of facilitation. All of this was in service of providing teachers with the knowledge and skills Lipman thought were necessary for them to be effective teachers of philosophy for children.

This explains why Lipman's novels make good choices for teachers with little or no philosophical background but a desire to incorporate philosophy into their classrooms. They can gain the skills and knowledge they need through the materials and workshops available from Lipman's Institute.

Still, there are some issues with Lipman's novels. First, consider the mirroring process I have just pointed to. Although it is crucial to Lipman's belief that his novels will get students to engage philosophically, he unfortunately does not present a defense of his view. As Kenneth B Kidd points out, this is a serious lacuna: "Lipman and his associates also assumed that students would identify with and emulate the characters in the novels, although they do not offer theories as to how or why that happens (or proof that it does)" (Kidd, 2020, p. 37). Given Lipman's insistence that novels designed for philosophy for children classes is the best way to introduce philosophy into elementary schools, a more compelling rationale for the effectiveness of this method needs to be given.

There are some other issues about Lipman's approach that are also worth considering. The first involves the issue of imposition. Despite his express desire to let the children set the agenda for their discussions, Lipman's novels are designed to raise very specific philosophical problems for the children to discuss. In this way, he seems to go against his own recommendation to allow the children to discuss what they want.

More worrying is the fact that the philosophical issues that Lipman includes in his novels are ones that *he* recognizes as distinctly philosophical. Only problems that Lipman has already identified as philosophical are presented in his texts. Karin Murris (2015) in particular thinks that Lipman's choice of philosophical topics to raise in discussion is biased by his interest in pragmatism and Analytic philosophy. She is particularly upset by his exclusion of issues central to the Continental tradition of philosophy. She believes that this bias has caused some European philosophers to reject his model.

Despite the differences in their approaches, Gareth Matthews is liable to similar criticisms. Matthews also writes stories for his dialogues with children, but these stories are tied to classical philosophical texts, usually Platonic dialogues or Aristotelian treatises. Matthews transforms these texts into discussions featuring young people, much in the manner of Lipman. And like Lipman, Matthews constructs his dialogues around issues that he has found in such standard philosophical works as Plato's *Gorgias* (see Matthews, 2008, p. 34ff).

The problem with both of these philosophers' procedures is that they limit the range of potential issues that children cannot discuss in their philosophy sessions to those that are widely acknowledged as philosophical in the Analytic tradition of philosophy. Analytic philosophy developed during the early twentieth century through the impact of formal logic on traditional philosophy. While dominant in graduate education in English-speaking countries, Analytic philosophy is not the only contemporary form of philosophy.

So-called Continental philosophy is a very different tradition for doing philosophy that focuses on different issues. Those concerns get short shrift in the Lipman-Matthews corpus.

This worry does not show that books written specifically for doing philosophy with children can't include a wider range of philosophical issues. And, indeed, philosophers like David Kennedy have attempted to do just that (Kennedy, 2019 and 2012). His novel, *Dreamers* (2019), attempts to employ the perspective of post-humanism in its presentation of the distinction between the human and the non-human.

Attempts such as Kennedy's can help enlarge the scope of philosophical issues addressed in novel expressly written for philosophical discussions. It marks a hopeful trend. It remains to be seen whether such books attain the popularity of Lipman and Matthews' books and stories, and how they embody philosophical issues not acknowledged in the Analytic tradition.

4.3 The Trouble with *Harry*

My own worries about philosophical novels developed specifically to teach children philosophy were heightened as the result of an attempt to teach Lipman's work to my own college students. Because I found a theatrical adaptation of Chapter 5 of *Harry* written by Steve Williams, I decided to use that chapter as the example of Lipman's methodology.[3] I had the students volunteer to read the various parts. My students enjoyed acting out the different roles, but something struck me as I listened to them reading the dialogue aloud that I hadn't picked up on before.

In Chapter 5—in what follows I discuss Lipman's book, not Williams' adaptation—Harry is with his friends Mark and Maria, as they discuss a history course that Mark thinks is boring. Harry agrees, saying that some of the courses in their school are boring while others are not. Mark responds that all of the courses are boring.

In response, Harry's friend Maria states, "if some courses are *uninteresting*, then it must be that there are other courses that are *interesting*" (Lipman, 1971, p. 21). Maria is here drawing an inference, thereby engaging in the type of reasoning that philosophical logic aims to regulate. Roughly, she has engaged in reasoning of the form, "If some x are not p, then some x are p." This is a fallacious inference and it prompts Harry to give Maria a lesson in logic:

> It doesn't follow, Maria," Harry objected. "Look," he said, taking from his pocket the bag of candies, which was still almost full. "Suppose you didn't know what kind of candy was in the bag. And then you saw me take out three pieces of candy, and they were all brown. Would it follow that there were other pieces still in the bag that weren't brown?
>
> (*Lipman, 1971, pp. 21–22*)

A moment later, Harry gives the conclusion to their discussion:

> If all you know is that some of the candies in the bag are brown, you can't say what color they all are, and you certainly can't say, because some are brown, that some must not be!
>
> (*Lipman, 1971, pp. 21–22*)

At this point, the discussion shifts to the topic of prejudice, and how people jump to conclusions.

This entire passage may seem unproblematic. After all, in this passage, Maria makes a claim: you can infer from the statement "some courses in our school are uninteresting" the statement that "some courses are interesting." Harry objects to this claim and attempts to get Maria to see that she does not understand a basic logical principle and has, in fact, committed a logical fallacy.

There is one feature of this interchange that struck me as I watched my students reading the scene. Here was a boy telling a girl that she had made a mistake and presenting her with a thought experiment to show her why she was wrong. The recent term "mansplaining" conceptualizes the problems with this. It's not just a problem with Harry or Lipman's book, but a more widespread cultural issue about men and their gender privilege. Given that our awareness of gender issues is certainly stronger now than it was in 1971, we have good reason to eschew using a book that employs such a problematic representation of gender roles for teaching young students.

There is also a deeper, more theoretical problem with Harry's claims.[4] It is one that many beginning students of philosophy fall prey to. They use their new-found knowledge of logic to browbeat other students in a way that borders on intellectual bullying. Unfortunately, Lipman replicates this objectionable behavior in this section of *Harry*. I will have to provide a bit of background to explain it. (For those interested, I have included a technical appendix at the end of this chapter that uses logical notation to explain Harry's argument. But I will explain the issue without recourse to formalism here.)

In the early decades of the twentieth century, philosophers discovered a new field of philosophy, the philosophy of language. Using developments in philosophical logic, philosophers like Bertrand Russell and Ludwig Wittgenstein attempted to understand ordinary language as having an implicit logical structure. The idea was that by revealing the logical structure of language, philosophers would be able to avoid many mistakes made by their predecessors. Wittgenstein's first book, *Tractatus Logico-Philosophicus*, is an example of a philosophical text that attempts to regulate our normal use of words through by employing logical regimentation.

This approach to language has been criticized by philosophers who embrace the approach known as ordinary language philosophy. Such philosophers have objected to treating our normal ways of speaking as concealing fallacies that the knowledgeable philosopher is able to reveal. Philosophers like the Ludwig Wittgenstein of *The Philosophical Investigations*, JL Austin, and Paul Grice have attempted to show the problems inherent in the attempt to use logic to clarify the meaning of natural language expressions.

Harry follows the Russell-early Wittgenstein program of treating language as having an implicit logical structure that needs to be revealed. He takes Maria to have made a fallacious inference and he employs a thought experiment to show her why her claim is ill-founded. He believes that she mistakenly concluded from the claim that some of the classes in their school are not interesting that some of them are. It is a fallacious inference because of its form, and has nothing to do with the actual question of whether any classes in the school are not boring.

The problem that emerged as I listened to my students reciting their parts is that Harry ignores an important aspect of our use of language: communication takes place in concrete situations in which we use meaningful expressions, that is, statements with literal meaning, to convey our thoughts to others. In so doing, we move beyond the literal meaning of those expressions to convey what Grice calls "speaker's meaning," that is, what the speaker intends his listener to understand by his or her utterance (Grice, 1989, esp. pp. 22–40). In his response to Maria, Harry treats her statement as if it were occurring in a logic text, not in an actual conversation and Lipman manifests no qualms about that.

But our linguistic interactions with others cannot be understood as simply embodying the norms of logical inference. For example, when we are listening to someone speak, a normative presupposition that guides our interpretation of their statements is that they always make the *strongest* statement possible. What "strongest" means in this context is that a speaker who makes a statement will always try to make the most inclusive claim that they can possibly make. In the current context, this means that making a statement about "some" members of a set—here, the set of all the classes at the school—entails that the speaker doesn't believe that the relevant "all" statement is true. Such norms are part of the *pragmatics* of our use of language.

Returning to Maria's claim, when she says "Some of the classes are uninteresting," our speech pragmatics dictate that she does not believe herself able to claim that "All of the classes are uninteresting." As I have said, this is not part of the literal meaning of the statement she makes, but it is part of the pragmatics of her using those words to communicate to Harry and Mark. This means she is perfectly justified in claiming that some of the classes must be interesting, for it follows from the pragmatics of the situation in which she (and Mark) claim that some of the classes are not interesting.

As I mentioned earlier, it was only while listening to my students act out this scene from *Harry* that I realized that it contained some objectionable elements: it not only conveyed an unacceptable gender dynamic between Harry and Maria, but it also presented Harry as justified in his criticism of her reasoning. In listening to the play, I realized that Maria was not making the fallacious inference that Harry attributes to her; rather, if we understand the context in which she makes the claim, we can see what she intends to say and why it is perfectly appropriate.

Now, Lipman is a good philosopher. While he may not have been as sensitive to gender issues as he should have been, he certainly was knowledgeable about the philosophy of language. How could he have included such a problematic incident in his novel?

I have concluded that the problem in Lipman's presentation of this incident is indicative of a broader worry about using books that are explicitly written to teach children a philosophical view: the problem is that the author's interest in getting children to understand a view prevents them from seeing the problems in their presentation of it. Lipman was so intent on showing children the importance of valid principles of inference—and invalid ones—that he overlooked the possibility that Maria had actually reasoned in a perfectly acceptable manner. In the chapter we have been examining, Lipman is only concerned with issues regarding valid inferences and not with the pragmatics of our natural language. As he attempts to get the children reading the book to understand principles of logic, he uses an example of a speech situation that philosophers now realize is governed by principles other than simply those of first-order logic.

So, a book written to explicitly teach philosophy to children may suffer from its author's attempt to demonstrate the validity of a particular philosophical theory even though that theory may not apply adequately to the situation being depicted in the book's narrative. I don't claim to have done an exhaustive study of books explicitly written to introduce children to philosophy, so I can't say how widespread this problem is. I can only say that it is one reason to be wary of using such novels in a classroom.

Of course, a philosophically sophisticated reader of *Harry* could do as I have done, and critique the book's presentation of gender and Harry's argument. But most teachers are not in a position to do the latter, for they do not have the in-depth knowledge of developments in twentieth-century philosophy of language required to critique the philosophy behind Lipman's narrative. As a result, the problematic aspects of the story will remain unchallenged.

My discussion here highlights one of the risks of using philosophical novels expressly designed to raise philosophical questions. The problematic features of the text may escape a facilitator's notice, so they may encourage their students to embrace suspect or outmoded ideas. While this does not require us to completely eschew using such books, it is important for practitioners to become cognizant of the problematic features of such texts.

It is also worth remembering that one of the central rationales for teaching young children philosophy was to enhance their sense of wonder at the world. Lipman's novels rarely convey this sense of wonder, though later novels like *Kia and* are less didactic than *Harry*, and so less likely to fall into the error I have been discussing. For this reason, we need to consider other ways to introducing philosophy to the young, as I do in the next chapter when I discuss picture books.

Appendix 4.1. Technical

There is a rule of logic that Chapter 5 of *Harry* is structured to get children to understand. In order for it to be applicable to the ordinary language discussion that Maria and Harry have, the standard interpretation of some logical symbols have to be understood. Most importantly, the word "some" gets interpreted via the existential quantifier "(Ex)" which says that "there is an x such that..." and the word "all" via the universal quantifier "(Ax)" which says "for all x...." Maria's statement that "if some courses are *uninteresting*, then it must be that there are other courses that are *interesting*" gets translated as follows:

$$(Ex) \sim Ix \rightarrow (Ex)Ix$$

where "$\sim$" is the sign for negation or not, "$\rightarrow$" is the sign for material implication or "if...then," and "I" stands for the word "interesting."

Anyone familiar with first-order logic—that's what these symbols are used in—knows that the general principle Maria proposes and that I have symbolized above is not valid. Given the use of the existential quantifier as a translation of the English term "some," it is immediately obvious that you can't infer from the fact that some members of a group have a property that other members must lack it.

So, from the point of view of first-order logic, Harry is perfectly justified in what he says. But the discussion between Harry and Maria takes place in English and is governed by a set of principles other than those of formal logic. That's why there is a problem with Harry's objections to Maria's claim.

Notes

1 Because Lipman's novel was initially circulated privately, there is disagreement on the exact date of its publication.
2 Lipman (1989), chapter 6, section 3, lines 5–19.
3 The play was written by Steve Williams and can be found here: https://p4c.com/wp-content/uploads/2016/03/RT-Harry-Stottlemeiers-Discovery.pdf. Accessed on October 28, 2020.
4 In the chapter in his instruction manual on chapter 5 of *Harry*, Lipman identifies the problem that Harry is raising differently than I have. He claims the issue is one about inductive reasoning, that is, moving from specific cases to a broader generalization (Lipman et al., 1984, pp. 112 ff). This seems to me a misrepresentation of what actually transpires in the discussion between Harry and Maria.

5

THE ADVANTAGES OF PICTURE BOOKS

I have always used picture books to begin the discussions I have facilitated for young children. There are a number of reasons for this. One was that, in Massachusetts, teachers were already required to teach picture books in their classes by the Massachusetts Curriculum Frameworks (https://www.doe.mass.edu/frameworks), so that I could get philosophy into their classrooms without adding a new subject to their already crowded curricula. I was only suggesting a different method for teaching the books they were already using.

Another was that the philosopher who introduced me to philosophy for children, Gareth Matthews, thought picture books raised significant philosophical issues. He had developed some materials for teachers to use in teaching these books.[1] I saw myself as carrying on in his footsteps.

What I didn't realize during my initial forays into working with children was that the originator of the movement, Matthew Lipman, was opposed to using picture books. Lipman's opposition to picture books stemmed, at least in part, from claims he made about the relationship between the words and images in a picture book and other children's literature. After considering Lipman's argument for his stance, I will use Maurice Sendak's *Where the Wild Things Are* (1963) to show why Lipman is wrong. *Pace* Lipman, picture books make great vehicles for getting children interested in discussing philosophy precisely because their combination of words and images make them a unique artform, one that engages children both emotionally and cognitively.

5.1 Lipman's Argument

From the very beginning of his development of philosophy for children, Lipman opposed using picture books to introduce young children to philosophy.[2] He

DOI: 10.4324/9781003257455-7

broaches this subject during a discussion of fairy tales in the book he co-authored with Ann Margaret Sharp and Frederick S Oscanyan. He contrasts picture books with both science and his own philosophical novels. He begins by noting that fairy tales are written for children by adults, certainly not a controversial observation, though it does obscure the oral tradition from which written fairy tales evolved. While Lipman's claim about the authorship of fairy tales might appear innocuous, he thinks it's not. Remarking on the stories that parents make up to tell their children, Lipman says, "The parent who invents stories for children nonetheless runs the risk of so indulging his own imagination as to preempt the child's imagination" (Lipman et al., 1980, p. 35).

The concern that adults could usurp children's imaginations is a central concern in Lipman's denigration of picture books. It is, nonetheless, odd. I assume that most parents tell their children made-up stories, for example, at bedtime to get their children to sleep in response to a child's request: "Daddy, Mommy, tell me a story." It's hard to understand why Lipman believed a child's imagination would be stifled by hearing a made-up tale, especially since they have to listen and imagine the storyworld created as their parents tell them a story. Lipman provides no reason to justify his claim.

Instead, he continues in the same vein, emphasizing the danger that grown-ups telling children stories poses to their children's imaginative lives. "But to what extent," he asks rhetorically, "do we rob children of *their* creativity by doing their imagining for them?" (Lipman et al., 1980, p. 35) Once again, this is a very strange claim. What exactly are the imaginings that we "rob" children of? Do children possess certain imaginary scenarios that telling them a story destroys? How could this threaten their creativity? These problematic claims receive virtually no justification from Lipman.

The closest Lipman comes to explaining his view occurs as he is justifying his decision to eschew the use of illustrations in his philosophical novels: "We have resisted putting illustrations in the children's books we publish because we feel that to do so is to do for children what they should do for themselves: provide the imagery that accompanies reading and interpretation" (Lipman et al., 1980, pp. 35–36).

Joanna Haynes and Karin Murris have argued that Lipman's claim conflates imagery with imagination (2012, pp. 66–68).[3] I take them to be distinguishing the imagery that is present in the illustrations of a picture book or even a chapter book from the imaginative work that is required to understand a story. Because Lipman does not amplify his statement, it's hard to know what exactly he thinks a child *loses* when they read an illustrated book.

There is something else that is even more puzzling in Lipman's contention. He claims that the pictures in an illustrated story deprive a child of the opportunity to imagine the characters on their own and that children ought to have the chance to do just that. It is true that a child reading *Alice's Adventures in Wonderland* (1865) will likely imagine that Alice looks like the girl pictured in John Tenniel's wonderful illustrations. This means that they will take Alice to be a young, white girl with blonde hair.[4] Does this fact justify Lipman's contention that the illustrations of such books rob the children of the opportunity to imagine for themselves?

I think not. We would do better to see pictures like Tenniel's of Alice as providing children with some of the materials they need to fully imagine the events described in the book. Once a child has seen a picture of Alice, they can better imagine her undergoing the adventures that she does. Such imagining is a complex process that involves integrating written text and pictures into a coherent narrative. This "imaginative" work requires children to do a lot of mental processing, using not just their imaginations but other cognitive skills and background knowledge they possess.

In addition, the illustrations in picture books provide a great deal of entertainment for both child and adult readers of the book. Increasingly, picture book illustrators are being recognized as artists, for their work deserves to be taken seriously as it is, for example, in the Eric Carle Museum of Picture Book Art in Amherst, Massachusetts. The illustrations also give a child the sense that the story they are reading is "real," for the pictures suggest that there is a fictional world inhabited by the beings pictured in the illustrations. All of this helps *stimulate* rather than suppress a child's imagination.

In general, Lipman seems to have a very rudimentary and quite inadequate understanding of the relationship between the images and the words in a picture book. While some picture books have images that simply picture the events related by the words, in general that is not the case. Often, the story presented in a picture book is not fully determined by the words, the text. The illustrations in picture books then play a substantive role in creating the story that is told in the book. A reader of such books has to interpret the images and see how they contribute to the developing story. When this occurs, it makes no sense to assert that children should provide the information necessary to complete a story presented by the words in the book by providing "imagery" on their own. That's not how the illustrations in picture books work.

We therefore need to think about whether anything can be said in general about the relationship between words and images in a picture book. I turn to that task in the next section of this chapter.

5.2 Words and Images in a Picture Book

Picture books are one example of illustrated books, that is, books that contain images as well as words. This is not the place to develop a complete account of the nature of illustrated books.[5] Nonetheless, some general observations will be helpful.

There are at least three basic types of illustrated books: illustrated novels, picture books, and comics, of which graphic novels are a particular kind. For ease of reference, I use the term "illustrated novels" as a general term to refer to illustrated literary works that are generally intended for adult consumption. It will include, in addition to illustrated novels proper, illustrated books of poetry and illustrated versions of other texts like *The Bible* and epics like Dante's *Divine Comedy*. Most contemporary novels do not have images in them, but this was not always the case. Especially in the nineteenth century, illustrated novels were quite common. For example, Charles Dickens' *Pickwick Papers* was initially serialized by Chapman and Hall in 1836 and 1837. Initially, Dickens had to construct his narrative from pictures that were already drawn, but he soon wrote text that his illustrators had to illustrate. Most illustrated novels, however, begin with a written text the illustrators use as the basis for their pictures.

In general, the pictures in illustrated novels are dependent upon the text they accompany. The text creates a story world to which the pictures need to be faithful. The primacy of the written text is an important characteristic of such works.

Illustrated novels thus employ images that are genuine *illustrations* of their stories, for the story is essentially determined by the words, the text. The images play a supplementary role in that they refer to events and settings determined by the words of the book.

"Comics" is a general term that includes the strips that populate the funny pages of daily newspapers, comic books, or soft cover volumes that feature characters from the daily strips, and so-called graphic novels. I say "so-called" for many of these books are actually memoirs, such as *Maus* and *Fun Home*. The different types of comics share the basic structure of a sequence of panels in which words and images occur. This differentiates them from illustrated novels that have no general structure for the images they include.

There are a number of fundamental differences between the images in comics and in illustrated books. First is the style used in the illustrations. While the images that adorn novels and other literature intended for adults are often realistic, those found in comic books are not. Because of the technology for the reproduction of comics in newspapers required the use of Ben-Day dots, the images found in comics involve a great deal of abstraction.[6] There is generally little attempt to create an illusory three-dimensional space into which the characters are placed, although there are times when the images do make that attempt.

The words and images in a comic generally have a different relationship than that present in illustrated novels. This is because a comic generally does not include much text other than direct speech represented by a speech balloon or a similar device. (Some comics do include a great deal of narration, but they are the exception that proves the rule.) For this reason, the images in a comic provide a great deal of information that cannot be treated as secondary, simply an illustration of events and settings described in the comic's text. A comic's images are more fundamental than that. The narrative of a comic is *co-determined* by the words and the images working together.

Picture books fall between these two types of illustrated books. The relationship between the words and images occurring in them does not fit into a single model. Some of them are like illustrated novels in that their images are illustrations of events and characters described verbally in the text; others resemble comics in that the images do more than provide illustrations of characters and scenes described verbally. There is also no limitation on the nature of the images such as there is in comics due to the use of the Ben-Day dots. In fact, the creativity of the illustrators of picture books is one reason for their popularity.

The variety of styles employed in picture books is quite amazing. The fantastic (in both sense of the word) illustrations that populate the books of Dr. Seuss (Theodor Geisel) are one reason why his books have been so incredibly popular.[7] The use of collage, one of the great artistic innovations in the early part of the twentieth century, is also an important feature of many picture books, from the wonderful stories of Eric Carle to the glorious creations of Leo Lionni. These are just some examples of the styles used in picture book illustrations.

Some picture books, like illustrated novels, employ illustrations of their written texts. Even in such cases, the illustrations provide more information than that included in the text. This is due to the difference between verbal descriptions and visual images. While the former need only have a few details—"suddenly a white rabbit with pink eyes ran close by her …. The Rabbit actually took a watch out of its waistcoat pocket" (Carroll, pp. 25–26)—the illustration of this short passage must include many features not mentioned in the text such as the rabbit's ears, legs, and arms. Pictures have no alternative but to supplement the verbal description of a character or event so as to make it possible to visually represent what the words describe.

Other picture books give their pictures a much more substantive role in the creation of the fictional world of the work. I will provide a detailed examination of one such picture book in a moment. For now, it will suffice to acknowledge that picture books, like comics, can have images that work hand in hand with their verbal text to create the fictional world of the work.

Despite having an academic specialty in aesthetics, Lipman gives no indication of having any acquaintance with or theoretical understanding of picture books and the logic of the relationship between their texts and images. It is only because of this that he can make the dismissive comments he does about their illustrations. I now will examine one picture book in detail in order to show that the images it contains play a substantive role in the development of the book's narrative and encourage the imaginations of its readers.

5.3 Word and Image in *Where the Wild Things Are*

Maurice Sendak's Caldecott Medal winning *Where the Wild Things Are* (1963) has been cited as the first contemporary picture book.[8] There are many reasons that can support this claim, including the style and importance of the illustrations and the lack of clear closure in the book's ending. Even if one disagrees with this judgment, there is no doubt that Sendak's book represents a high point in the art of the picture book, both as a result of its ambiguous narrative and its amazing images.

I am going to analyze the way in which the images in *Where the Wild Things Are* work together with the words to construct the book's story. Because the images play an essential role in this regard, we will see the reductive nature of Lipman's contention about the relationship between imagery and the imagination in picture books. As a result, we will realize that there are no "in principle" reasons to reject picture books as useful tools for philosophy discussions with elementary-school children.

The story presented in *Where the Wild Things Are* is deceptively simple. Max, a young boy, has been misbehaving. This results in his mother calling him a "wild thing," to which Max responds by telling her he will "eat her up." This is the last straw as far as she is concerned, so she sends Max to bed without his supper. The despondent Max goes to his room where, before long, a forest grows. Max then decides to sail to the Land Where the Wild Things are. He embarks on a sea voyage and eventually winds up in the Land of the Wild Things. They make him their king and a large rumpus ensues. After a while, Max gets tired of being with them and, when he smells food, decides to return home to where "someone loves him best." After another long sea voyage, Max is back in his room where his dinner, still hot, awaits him. The end.

I have characterized the book narrative as "deceptively simple." Once they have finished the book, a perceptive reader will note that there are some discrepancies in what the narrative has established that need to be resolved. For example, when Max sails off, he sails "through night and day, and in and out of weeks, and almost over a year." His return trip takes a similar amount of time, and yet, when he returns to his room, his dinner is still hot, so that very little time can have elapsed. Can we resolve the apparent contradictions in the story of Max's sojourn?

The contradictions disappear with the realization that Max has been dreaming or imagining everything that happens in his room. A forest grows in it only because Max imagines (or dreams) that it has. His adventures with the Wild Things are again the product of his quite vivid imagination and hence "subjective," as opposed to real events that occur in the "objective" world of the story such as Max's being sent to his room. Making this distinction between events that actually take place in the world of the story and ones that only take place in Max's imagination is the key to resolving the apparent contradictions in the story and its pictures. Anyone reading the book has to supply key interpretive moves in order to render the narrative coherent.

The book provides many clues to secure our interpretation of the central images of the book as representing the contents of Max's consciousness. On the second spread (a spread consists of the two pages one views when the book is open), as Max is shown chasing his dog with a large fork in his hand, a picture Max drew hangs on the wall. It is just a single face drawn in pencil but in a manner that foreshadows the pictures we see later of the Wild Things. The fact that Max has made this drawing suggests that the pictures of the Wild Things we later see are, in fact, the products of Max's imagination because they resemble his drawing so closely. In addition, many features of Max's experience with the Wild Things are inverted versions of his experience with his mother. At one point, for example, he gets frustrated with them, so, like his mother, he sends them to bed without their supper. This role inversion happens a number of times during Max's stay with the Wild Things, as when they say that they don't want him to leave and will *eat him up* because they love him so, thereby mimicking the transgression that led to Max's punishment. And this allows Max to play the role of parent to the disobedient Wild Things.

This distinction between real and imaginary events portrayed in the book applies to the book's illustrations. The images we see once Max has been sent to his room are not images of events taking place in the objective world depicted in the story—its "real" world—but rather images that depict the content of his imagination. Only in the book's final spread, when we see Max return to his room, do the images once again show us actual events taking place in the story's objectively real world, just as they did at the book's outset.

This bifurcation of the images of the book between ones depicting the real world and ones depicting the content of Max's imagination marks a genuine innovation by Sendak. The only other book I know of that approaches this sort of complex strategy of illustration is *Harold and the Purple Crayon* by Crockett Johnson (1955). In that book, we see Harold drawing things with his purple crayon. Once he has drawn something, it becomes "real" and thus part of his world, something Harold has to contend with as the story develops. So, for example, once Harold has drawn an ocean, he has to be careful not to drown in it! But as imaginative and wonderful as that book is, its images lack the complexity and beauty of those in *Where the Wild Things Are*, for *Harold*'s pictures are more or less what a child of Harold's age might draw.

What Sendak has done in the pictures of Max's adventures is to find a visual analogue for the mental life of a child. It's a truism to say that children have rich imaginative lives; but Sendak does more than convey to his audience the validity of this truism. He has created images that *show* reader-viewers the contents of a child's mind as he responds to what he thinks is the unfair punishment his mother has meted out. Whether Max is dreaming or just creatively imagining his journey, Sendak provides us with a means to access Max's subjective experience, something not ordinarily done in a picture book.

My contention earlier was that the images in a picture book like *Where the Wild Things Are* work in tandem with the words to create the book's narrative. Without the pictures of the Land of the Wild Things, a reader-viewer would not discover that the story of Max's adventures take place mainly in his mind, not in "objective reality."

Even more interesting from the point of view of the theory of picture books is how some of the images in the book play a significant role *on their own*. Consider the first spread of Max arriving in the Land of the Wild Things. On the left extreme, we see Max in his boat, still wearing his wolf costume with a frown on his face. In the fantastical landscape ahead of him there are four Wild Things. The book says "they roared their terrible roars and gnashed their terrible teeth and rolled their terrible eyes and showed their terrible claws," so that we might conclude, in the absence of the images, that the Wild Things are really scary creatures.

The images, however, undermine what the book explicitly states. Although the Wild Things do have pointy claws and large teeth, they are not very scary. While we can't hear what they sound like, their yellow eyes are large and round. In fact, the Wild Things look very much like stuffed animals. Despite some features that might have made them scary, the overall impression given by the pictures of them is that they are cute, lovable monsters who one would like to hug, not creatures to run from in fear. The images of the Wild Things undercut the scary message the words would convey on their own.

The role of the pictures becomes even more important a little later in the story. After Max has been made "King of all Wild Things," he cries, "let the wild rumpus start." The three spreads that follow have no words on them at all. Instead, we just see pictures of the four or five Wild Things and Max having their rumpus. They howl at the moon, swing from trees, and take part in a grand parade with King Max riding on the back of one of the Wild Things.

Rather than undercutting children's ability to imagine, these three spreads help them imagine a "wild rumpus" in ways they could not without them. We see Max having a great time with the Wild Things as they play with one another. Had the book just said, "then Max played with the Wild Things and even had a parade," it would be so much less rich and children would not be inspired to imagine the Land of the Wild Things with anything like the creativity that Sendak employed. At the most fundamental level, the pictures function to amplify and develop the very sketchy ideas put forward by the text.

Once we have reevaluated the book's story by attributing the middle section of the book to Max's imagination, we are in a position to think about what the story really means. At the beginning of the story, Max is clearly acting up. He responds to his mother's punishment with anger, as the scowl on his face indicates. That picture of the scowling Max is the only indication of what his response is, another example of the important role the pictures have in creating the story. At the end of the story, the smiling Max is glad to be home, as he sees the food his mother has left for him. He has indeed wound up "where someone loved him best of all."

In his room during his imaginary voyage, Max works through his emotions. In order to do so, he externalizes and objectifies the very emotions that led him to act out. The Wild Things, from this point of view, are an externalization of the emotions Max experiences that get him into trouble and that he cannot easily control. As "King of the Wild Things," however, he gets to control the Wild Things, by, for example, sending them to bed without their supper. This allows him to "work through" those emotions, making it possible for him to acknowledge his desire to return home.

Max's progress from anger to an acknowledgment of his mother's love, then, involves a working through of his emotional response to his mother's punishment.[9] The working through is what is presented through the words and images that depict Max's sojourn in the land of the Wild Things. Through his taking on the roles his mother had played and projecting his own feelings onto the Wild Things, Max is able to leave behind his anger and become the loving child he must generally have been. Our understanding of the pictures plays a vital role in allowing us to understand the book's narrative and meaning.

While there is a lot more to say about *Where the Wild Things Are*, I have said enough to confirm two claims I made earlier in relation to Lipman's dismissal of picture books as inappropriate to use for philosophizing with children. First, the illustrations are not doing work that would be better left to children but are part and parcel of this book's narrative. We don't perceive them passively but need to actively interpret them, seeing how the work with the text to create a consistent story. Second, the illustrations play an essential role in this narrative; it would not be possible to tell this particular story without its illustrations. They both create the ambiguity necessary for the narrative and provide a way to disambiguate it.

The appropriate conclusion to draw is that there are no reasons to judge it inappropriate to use pictures together with words in a book for children. Rather than seeing the images as undermining children's ability to imagine, we have examined one picture book in which they play an important role, one that stimulates rather than stultifies children's imaginations. The manner in which the pictures work together with the words in *Where the Wild Things Are* is representative of the role that images play in picture books.

5.4 Conclusion

If we compare *Harry Stottlemeier's Adventure* with *Where the Wild Things Are* in regard to their suitability as stimuli for philosophical discussions, a number of things emerge. First, there is a lot more material that a would-be facilitator could avail themself of to prepare to teach *Harry*. The nearly 500-page manual *Philosophical Inquiry*, contains exercises, lesson plans, and many other materials that could be useful to someone wanting to use *Harry* as the basis for philosophy lessons.

Although there are no such materials available for *Wild Things*, this does not automatically make it less useful as a stimulus for philosophical dialogues. In fact, the book has many advantages. Perhaps the primary one is that it is much more appealing to young people than Lipman's novel. They are much more likely to be engaged in the attempt to unpack the meaning of the story than they are to discuss the problems with Maria's claim that some of the classes in her school are boring. Picture books engage students more fully than philosophical novels do.

In addition, more young people are likely to be engaged by *Wild Things*. While some students might find the intellectual puzzle at the heart of chapter 5 of *Harry* interesting to discuss, others may be turned off by its excessively intellectuality. They are much more likely to find Max's fate of having gone to bed without dinner—one that they may have shared with him—much more engaging to think about. In addition, the wonderful illustrations also engage readers and get them invested in unpacking their unusual function in the story.

Finally, we should recall the grounds I adduced in the first part of this book for introducing philosophy to young people. The one I want to emphasize here is *wonder*. When young people engage in a philosophical discussions, they should be energized by their wonder at features of the world and their experience. A skillful children's author and illustrator like Sendak can engage that sense of wonder by, among other things, recreating a child's subjective experience of the world. Seeing the Land of the Wild Things—even if it is only a product of Max's overheated imagination and not a real place—can foster a child's sense of wonder at the world and all it contains.

The same cannot be said for *Harry*. Despite such novels raising philosophical issues in a clear manner, they do not elicit wonder to the same degree as picture books. The charm and humor so evident in picture books is simply missing from such novels.

Since I have also rebutted the philosophical objections to using picture books in philosophical discussions with and among young children, I conclude that picture books are an outstanding way to introduce philosophy to young people. In fact, it is not only the young people who enjoy picture books. I have used them successfully with college students and adults, and they have proven to be a reliable means for stimulating philosophical discussions.

Notes

1 These materials have recently been republished by the IAPC: https://www.montclair.edu/iapc/wise-owl/
2 Despite his claims about picture books, Lipman did ask Gareth Matthews to write a column in *Thinking*, the journal Lipman edited, about philosophically interesting picture books.
3 By the time he wrote *Kia and Gus*, Lipman's opposition to illustrations seems to have weakened, for there are two illustrations in this book. The illustrations are simple black and white drawings that purport to be of a whale but look pretty much like scribbles.
4 I take up the issue of whether such illustrations make the books hard for non-white children to enjoy in Chapter 7.
5 I make some tentative steps in the development of such a theory in my 2012 article.
6 For an exemplary discussion of the structure of comic images, see Scott McCloud (1993).
7 The controversy about Dr Seuss' use of racist stereotypes does not to my mind detract from the originality of his style of illustration, though it is a problem in some of his books.
8 The claim is attributed to "many literary critics" by Haynes and Murris (2012, p. 28).
9 Was Max's mother justified in sending him to his room without his dinner? Recent discussion of this type of punishment suggest that it is not. Jennifer L. Baker states: "Sending your child to bed without dinner is a cruel act that [doesn't] have the desired results. … I think parents are learning [that there are] other ways [to discipline] that work better and don't involve a lot of coercion and overpowering." https://www.healthyway.com/content/parenting-habits-that-didnt-age-well/. Accessed on December 10, 2020.

6

HOW PICTURE BOOKS ACTUALLY PHILOSOPHIZE

This chapter continues my discussion of why picture books are among the best ways to initiate philosophical discussions. First, I will show how a very simple picture book story can actually *do philosophy*. Then, I will show how a story can counter problematic assumptions that children have acquired from popular culture. The philosophical nature of picture books allows them to be a positive force in children's educations.

The notion that a children's story—and, indeed, a rather simple one at that—could actually be doing philosophy may seem odd, if not even outrageous. I completely understand that reaction. When I first started working with children's books in an elementary-school setting over 20 years ago, I didn't think of them as doing philosophy, even though I was using them to initiate philosophical discussions among elementary school children. But the more I worked with these books and the stories they contain, the more convinced I became that some of them actually presented philosophical ideas and theses, and that occasionally one contained a philosophical argument.

Although the discussion in this chapter may seem abstract and far removed from our practice as teachers of philosophy to pre-university students, I'll demonstrate that it is not. Understanding how picture books present philosophical ideas allows us to see more clearly both what philosophy is and how it can be taught to young children as well as to provide additional reasons why picture books are such an important resource for elementary-school philosophy teachers.

6.1 Exploring Bravery with Frog and Toad

"Dragons and Giants" is a very short, but quite brilliant story by Arnold Lobel. Before his untimely death from AIDS at the age of 54 in 1987, Lobel

DOI: 10.4324/9781003257455-8

won many honors, including the Caldecott Medal for the "most distinguished American picture book for children" in 1981, though not for one of his Frog and Toad books. There is even a charming Broadway musical, *A Year with Frog and Toad*, based upon the *Frog and Toad* series.[1]

The philosophical issue that "Dragons and Giants" raises concerns *bravery*. Philosophers generally consider bravery to be a *virtue*, that is, a positive character trait, something people ought to exemplify in their lives. As such, the discussion of it takes place in the field of ethics, which is concerned with issues of human conduct, how people ought to behave. In discussing bravery, "Dragons and Giants" raises an ethical issue.

Toad starts things off by making a claim about bravery that lies at the heart of the story's philosophical investigation. In one of the story's delightful illustrations, we see him holding the book of fairy tales he and Toad have been reading. He says that the people in the book are brave because "they fight dragons and giants and they are *never afraid*" (emphasis added). The well-known fairytale of "Jack and the Beanstalk" is a good example of the sort of story Toad must have in mind, for Jack never appears scared of the giant and even manages to repeatedly outwit him, getting money, the hen that laid the golden egg, and even a golden harp.

Although Toad is making a claim only about the people in the book, it is easy to see how it can be *generalized* into a philosophical one, especially because he has given a general reason why he thinks the people in the fairy-tales are brave, namely they never experience fear. It's pretty clear that Lobel intends Toad to have articulated a general claim—that brave people are never afraid—that will be the focus of the rest of the story. And it is this *philosophical thesis* that, in Lobel's inimitable way, the story undermines.

In response to Toad's statement, Frog and Toad wonder whether they are brave like the heroes in the fairytales. As a first attempt at answering this question, our erstwhile amphibian philosophers look in a mirror. Philosophically sophisticated readers might smile knowingly and shake their heads at the notion that bravery is something that can be seen in a mirror. Frog and Toad, on the other hand, agree that they do *look brave*, although it's not at all clear what about their appearance justifies their assessment.

At this point, "Dragons and Giants" has already presented with *two theses about bravery*:

1. Being brave is incompatible with being scared.
2. Whether someone is brave can be determined by how they look.

The first claim is explicitly stated by Toad and the second is affirmed by Frog's stating, after looking at himself and Toad in a mirror, they both look brave.

Although the story will focus on the first claim, the second is also a phil-osophical claim worth reflecting on, for the story immediately undermines it when Toad asks, "Yes, but are we?" This poses a very interesting philosophical question by means of putting forward a distinction: is there a difference between someone *looking brave* and their actually *being brave*? And this suggests some additional issues: is there a way that brave people look? Is the look of a New Zealand Maori warrior doing the haka, for example, the look of a brave person? How can you tell? What about firefighters? Or policemen? Often, children with whom I have discussed "Dragons and Giants" cite these sorts of people, ones whose jobs require them to confront very dangerous situations, as examples of brave individuals. Even if we agree that such people are brave, the question remains: is their bravery something that can be seen in their appearance? Do black rubber boots and yellow rain coats show that firefighters are brave? And does looking brave, if there is a way to tell how a brave person looks, mean a person really *is* brave? All of these issues emerge quickly and quietly from the story and can be used as the basis for philosophical discussions with children.

Frog and Toad realize that they can't tell by looking in the mirror whether they really are brave, so they attempt to resolve it by heading off to climb a mountain. The reason why they do, although it is not explicitly formulated in the story, is that climbing a mountain is an activity that is *dangerous* to engage in. It's as close as they can come to fighting dragons and giants. So, if they can climb the mountain and face whatever dangers they encounter without becoming scared, Frog and Toad will have evidence that they are indeed brave, at least according to Toad's initial claim about bravery.

In proceeding as they do, Frog and Toad implicitly mobilize the idea that bravery is something that is employed in dangerous situations. There are many different types of situations that we human beings are likely to face as we live our lives and the appropriate way to respond to them will be different. Being temperate or moderate, for example, is something one only needs to employ in a situation where there are things tempting one into intemperance; in my case, a large bowl of peanuts sitting in front of me is sufficient to require the moderation that I can't always manifest. Bravery similarly has a specific type of situation that makes it the appropriate response, viz. one in which there is a (perceived) danger.

On their hike, Frog and Toad come face to face with three dangerous situations. Such situations involve, as I have just noted, the sorts of circumstances in which bravery is called for. But being brave is not the only way to respond to danger. *Cowards* flee from dangerous situations, while *rash* or *foolhardy* people seek them out.[2] But before getting distracted by these and other interesting quandaries about the nature of bravery, let's see how our protagonists fare on their adventure.

The first danger they encounter is a large snake who greets them, "Hello, lunch!" What is the brave thing for them to do in this situation?

Frog and Toad *run* from the snake. When they do, are they being brave? Or should they stand there and ... what? Get eaten? Or maybe vainly struggle not to be eaten? The snake is larger, quicker, and stronger than they are. How can they act bravely without winding up as lunch for a hungry reptile?

Frog and Toad's response as they run from the snake returns us to the central question raised by the story, for Toad is shaking but manages to scream, "I am not afraid!" Whether he really is afraid may be an interesting interpretive question, but the question of whether his actually feeling fear would mean that he was not brave is a philosophical one, indeed the one upon which we and the story are focusing.

Is Toad's assertion—that brave people never feel fear—true? Or is fear a tip off that one is actually in a dangerous situation? Indeed, from an evolutionary point of view, doesn't the presence of a danger explain why we feel fear in the first place? Would we admire someone who never felt fear, who laughed off threats to his life as completely insignificant? Isn't it reasonable for Frog and Toad to be scared of a large snake who sees them as his next meal? And doesn't that fear fuel their very rational, hasty retreat in the face of such an extreme threat to their lives? Before answering these questions, I want to follow our heroes as they confront two additional dangers as they climb the mountain.

The second danger that confronts Frog and Toad is an avalanche. They escape from this danger by *jumping* from its path, this time with the trembling Frog yelling that he is not afraid as the two resume their journey.

Once again, we need to ask whether Frog and Toad's response to this danger secures the case against their being brave. One might think so, despite the fact that they are repeatedly asserting that they are not afraid. But what is the brave thing to do when you see huge boulders falling down a mountain headed straight toward you? Is the only way to demonstrate your bravery to stick around and be crushed while beating your chest and thundering in a Tarzan-like manner? That seems rash rather than brave.

What is the relationship between a brave person and a rash one? We've already considered the idea that fear helps us react appropriately in dangerous circumstances. Maybe one difference between a brave person and a rash one is that the brave person is motivated by the fear they feel while the rash one either does not feel scared or simply ignores the feeling. But this suggests that, contrary to Toad's claim, feeling fear might actually be one of the ingredients of bravery rather than an indication of its absence.

A third danger in the shape of a hawk soon threatens our heroes. For the second time, our cherished amphibians seem like they might become a meal for a larger and stronger creature. But, upon seeing the hawk, they jump under a rock and the hawk flies away, leaving them safe if not completely sound.

This brings to mind a new consideration: Frog and Toad have responded to the three dangers they face in three different ways. As we have just seen, faced with a hawk, they hide under a rock rather than running away or jumping aside, the two responses they had to the previous dangers they encountered. Don't these appropriately differential, nuanced responses show that they are reacting rationally in order to elude the hawk, who could just swoop down and eat them if they run from it? Does this show that thinking plays a role in bravery, a feature of it we have so far not acknowledged?

Frog and Toad have now reached the final episode in their journey. Having reached the summit and concluded their ascent, the two amphibians now yell in unison that they are not afraid as they rapidly run down the mountain to Toad's house. Toad hides under the covers trembling and shaking, while Frog shuts himself in the closet. And yet they tell each other how much they enjoy having a brave friend. The story ends with Lobel's laconic comment, "They stayed there [i.e. under the covers and in the closet] for a very long time, just feeling brave together."

Maybe the appropriate question to ask at this point is whether the two amphibians are deluded. After all, they appear to be scared by all the dangers they have faced and eluded. Doesn't this mean they are not brave and so are wrong when they characterize each other as brave? At the story's conclusion, we are confronted once more by the question of whether Toad's characterization of the heroes of the book of fairy tales as brave because they face dangerous situations without being afraid accurately posits the absence of fear as a *necessary condition* for bravery. That term only means that, if what Toad claims were true, the absence of fear would only be one aspect of bravery.

6.2 The Philosophy in "Dragons and Giants"

I began this chapter by saying that "Dragons and Giants" is an example of a story that actually does philosophy. All we have seen so far is that it raises a wide range of issues about bravery. We now need to ask whether the story reaches any conclusions about bravery. I think that it does and this is what accounts for my saying it really does do philosophy.

The first and most significant way that "Dragons and Giants" does philosophy—and we'll see that there are a number—is by demonstrating that Toad's claim about bravery is false. It does so in a brilliant manner, presenting *an inconsistent triad*. An inconsistent triad is a set of three statements or propositions, all of which cannot simultaneously be true but each of which we initially think might be. Our task as philosophical readers of the story is to decide which claim we should reject.

Here is the inconsistent triad:

A. Frog and Toad feel afraid.
B. Frog and Toad are brave.
C. Brave people are never afraid.

For these three statements to form an inconsistent triad, two conditions need to be met. First, there must be a reason to accept the *prima facie* truth of each of the three statements. To say that these statements are *prima facie* true is only to say that, on our initial inspection, we have reason to think they are true, although we admit that we might ultimately decide they are not. Second, the three statements must jointly entail a *contradiction*. Philosophers generally don't like contradictions, so if we find a set of statements entailing one, the conclusion is that they cannot all be true.[3] We have to reject one as false and thus avoid the contradiction. That's what it means for the statements to be inconsistent.

Let's investigate why these three statements form an inconsistent triad. We can begin with claim (A): Frog and Toad are afraid. I think that this is pretty clear from the story, especially its ending. They have faced three significant dangers, any one of which could kill them. Why shouldn't they be afraid of those threatening things? The only factor I see counting against it is Frog and Toad's repeated assertion that they are not afraid. But I think that we should see their disavowals as simply part of the humor of the story and their desire to prove to themselves that they are brave. We don't really need to take it at face value, especially when we see them trembling and hiding under the bed covers and in a closet. What other than fear could motivate such behavior?

Whether Frog and Toad are actually brave, the claim made in (B), is less certain. At the end of the story, each says of the other he is a brave friend, and the narrator characterizes them, perhaps ironically, as being brave together. So, the jury may be out on that one. But for the purposes of my argument, let's just provisionally accept the fact of their bravery, since the two amphibians characterize each other and themselves as brave, and they have actually managed to climb the mountain and elude the dangers they faced during their ascent. In support of this, I'll note that they did not let their fear overcome them and paralyze them, something that can happen in dangerous situations. Instead, they reacted pretty rationally, discriminating between the three situations and taking a course of action in each that was appropriate to it. I'd say that this militates in favor of their being brave.

(C) is the most philosophically interesting statement, the others being (at least fictionally, i.e., in terms of the story) empirical: brave people are never afraid. This is, as you will recall, the generalization of the claim Toad made as the result of reading the book of fairy tales. As readers, we tentatively accept this claim on the basis of Toad's saying so and I suggest we do so as well, at least for the moment in order to see how the inconsistent triad presented in the story functions.

We are now in a position to see why the three form an inconsistent triad. If (C) is true, it follows that Frog and Toad cannot both be afraid and brave. But that is precisely what (A) and (B) assert, respectively. So, the three statements cannot all be true simultaneously. They thus form an inconsistent triad.

To resolve the inconsistency, we need to deny the truth of one of the three claims. The beauty of the story is that we feel a temptation to deny both (A) and (B). After all, Frog and Toad claim that they are not afraid. Even if we don't finally accept their claim, we do have some reason to endorse it. Similarly, we are tempted to say that they are not brave, for they do not confront any of the dangers that they face.

The alternative to denying the truth of (A) or (B) is to deny the truth of (C), and this is the strategy I endorse and whose validity I am now going to argue for. The rhetorical questions and asides I used earlier were meant to suggest that fear is actually a component of bravery. If we take bravery to be the appropriate response to dangerous situations, it makes sense to see fear as the conscious marker that one is in the type of situation in which bravery is called for. The feeling of fear tips a person off to the presence of danger and hence of the need to do something to deal with it. Bravery is simply the appropriate character trait to employ in such situations and it is triggered by the fear that is experienced. Rather than being antithetical to bravery, fear is actually the emotion that calls it forth, registers that the situation requires one to be brave.

Paying careful attention to the narrative of "Dragons and Giants" has involved us in actually doing some fairly sophisticated philosophy. What I mean by this is that reading the story carefully and thinking about the issues it raises brings one face to face with a puzzle about bravery that can only be resolved by the sort of careful reasoning about inconsistent triads we have just engaged in. This story, then, actually asks that its readers to do some serious philosophical thinking to resolve the central question that it poses: can you be brave and still be afraid?

Along the way, the story has also made some interesting philosophical claims. For example, we saw "Dragons and Giants" make a distinction between being brave and merely appearing to be. A number of philosophical issues can be raised about the grounds for this distinction and criteria for distinguishing between the two. But rather than doing that, I now respond to a possible critical response to my interpretation of the story.

6.3 Responding to a Skeptical Attack

A skeptic might deny my assertion that "Dragons and Giants" is actually *doing philosophy*. What more can I say to support my view? What about the story qualifies it as philosophizing? After all, "Dragons and Giants" lacks many of the obvious features present in most philosophical texts and has many other features that most works of philosophy lack. Complex terminology is an example of the former and illustrations of the latter. In the face of this counter-evidence, how can I really maintain what I have about the story?

My assertion that "Dragons and Giants" should be viewed as doing philosophy can be justified by referring to two facts: first, it puts forward a genuinely philosophical claim and second, it presents a counter-example to it. That this should qualify the story as doing philosophy can be seen from a recent list of techniques that constitute contributions to philosophy. Sandy Goldberg, in a

Facebook post reprinted in *Daily Nous* (Weinberg, 2021), presented a list of such contributions that was augmented by readers. A number of philosophical contributions of "Dragon and Giants" are on the list: making useful distinctions (being versus appearing brave), counter-exampling an accepted theory (that brave people do not feel fear), and raising an interesting new question (can brave people feel fear?).

To support my claim, I want to look at a work that everyone admits is a genuine work of philosophy that does philosophy precisely because it considers a philosophical claim only to reject it by means of a counter-example. The work I have in mind is Plato's *Republic*. Now the *Republic* has a lot more philosophy in it than the piece I am going to discuss; nonetheless, even that one piece is an indication of its philosophical character.

Toward the beginning of the *Republic*, Polemarchus, one of Socrates' interlocutors, proposes that justice or morality is "rendering to each his due" (331e). This becomes the philosophical claim whose truth Socrates, the dialogue's protagonist, investigates. Socrates gets Polemarchus to agree that returning something you have borrowed to the person from whom you borrowed it is an example of a just act, for it is something that is due them.

Socrates then asks whether it would be just or moral to give back a gun to someone from whom you borrowed it if you knew they were going to use it to kill some innocent people. (I have updated the example, but kept its basic form intact.) Polemarchus is forced to agree that that is not moral, so that the proposed norm—morality is giving people what they are due—is not an adequate account of the actual nature of morality. The story that Socrates tells functions as a *counter-example* because the action of returning the gun is an instance of "giving someone what they are due" but we believe that doing so is not the moral thing to do. So, the proposed elucidation of morality fails.

This brief example presents the type of reasoning that takes place in the *Republic* that is indicative of its actually doing philosophy. The dialogue focuses on a general claim, a purported definition, and then presents a story whose point is prompting our intuition that the general definition fails in that imaginary case.

"Dragons and Giants" involves this very pattern of reasoning. It begins with a thesis, Toad's claim that being brave means never being afraid. It then presents the story of Frog and Toad's adventures on their hike, leaving the reader with the task of resolving the inconsistent triad I presented earlier. The best resolution of this inconsistency, I have suggested, requires us to acknowledge Frog and Toad's bravery despite their fear, so that Toad's thesis—that being brave requires not feeling fear—is false. But that means that the narrative of "Dragons and Giants" presents a counter-example to Toad's claim about bravery and fear being antithetical. And in virtue of the presence of this type of philosophical argument, we should recognize the story as making a clear philosophical point, as actually doing philosophy.

And that's one reason why a story like "Dragons and Giants" is such a good way to introduce children to philosophy. It's not just that you are giving *them* an opportunity to engage in a philosophical discussion, though you are doing that. You are also getting them to see the presence of philosophy in the story itself, so that they have before them an example of philosophical reasoning that they are able to reconstruct though their discussion.

Having given "Dragon and Giants" a lot of credit for the presence of philosophy in it, I have to make a qualification. At the same time that we acknowledge the presence of philosophy in "Dragons and Giants" we need to admit that, from a philosophical point of view, it is not really original. Unlike Plato's *Republic*, "Dragons and Giants" is not making claims about bravery that philosophers have not made before. Indeed, in his *Nicomachean Ethics*, Aristotle presents a theory of bravery some of whose features "Dragons and Giants" replicates (see Irwin, 2000, Book III). Among Aristotle's claims is that feeling the appropriate amount of fear is one component of bravery.

This lack of philosophical originality is hardly surprising. But it should not blind us to the significance of the story's achievement. In order to see this, we need to think a bit more about what young children, the primary audience for "Dragons and Giants," generally think about bravery.

Even at the time of the story's publication in 1979, young children were being fed images of brave people that suggested to them that it was inappropriate to be scared in dangerous situations. The fact that Toad developed his view from reading a book of fairy tales indicates that popular culture heroes are generally depicted as immune from fear. And in so far as young children learn from what they have read, seen, and heard, they will imbibe the lesson that it's not appropriate to be afraid when danger threatens. It's just this that "Dragons and Giants" takes on: the popular conception of heroism that requires heroes not to be afraid.

What I'm suggesting is that "Dragons and Giants" is both original and significant when viewed in the appropriate context. No, it's not an original piece of philosophizing, if we are thinking about works in the grand (or maybe not so grand, considering its racism, sexism, and eurocentrism) tradition of Western philosophy. But it is a very creative and original response to a culture that fails to see the appropriateness of being scared in dangerous situations and that teaches young children a false view of heroism.

This feature of "Dragons and Giants" provides another reason why picture books are such a great resource to use with young children. These stories have the potential to counter problematic views children imbibe from popular culture. Picture books can be a source of resistance to such problematic notions as that being brave entails that one not be scared. This critical potential of picture books allies them with philosophy as endeavors seeking to provide children with the resources to resist harmful messages inherent in popular culture.

6.4 A Positive Account of Bravery

So far, my discussion of the philosophy contained in "Dragons and Giants" has been primarily negative in the sense that Toad's attempt at a definition of bravery is shown to be inadequate. I'd now like to show that there are any more positive results that can be garnered from the story.

When I co-facilitated a discussion of this story together with a UMass undergraduate at the Martin Luther King Jr. School in Springfield, Massachusetts a few years ago, the second graders had a clear disagreement about whether Frog and Toad were brave. Most thought they weren't and pointed to them trembling at the end of the story. But a few of the children thought they were brave, so I asked them why. A girl who I will call "Shakira" replied that she thought they were brave because they "kept going." What she meant, she said, was that they didn't stop climbing the mountain even after they saw the snake and other dangers, but continued with their original quest. "That's why they were brave," Shakira continued. "They didn't stop but kept on going." She later added that bravery wasn't so much about how you *felt* but what you *did*, thereby shifting emphasis from feeling fear to one's response to one's fears.

In my earlier discussion, I did mention some features of the story that provide the evidence that Shakira based her view on. The central one is that Frog and Toad are not deterred from completing their hike because of the dangers they encounter. Indeed, encountering some danger is essential to the task they set for themselves, namely determining whether they are brave by seeing how they respond to the dangers they encounter on their hike. So, Shakira's claim that they are brave finds support by Frog and Toad's not giving in to their fear by abandoning their mission.

Shakira's response suggests a positive characteristic of bravery: *cautious perseverance in the face of danger and fear.* I'm not sure about giant killers and knights in shining armor, the sorts of people who fight dragons and giants, but ordinary human beings are brave when they don't let their fears keep them from doing what they know they need to do. This doesn't mean that one will never abandon a project when they discover how dangerous it actually is. As the saying goes, "discretion is the better part of valor," and that suggests that caution is needed. But when you do persevere in a course of action you realize is dangerous, you are being brave.

6.5 Conclusion

Here is a summary of the most important philosophical claims about bravery made by "Dragons and Giants." Its initial claim was that fear, rather than being antithetical to bravery, was a component of it, for a brave person can feel fear, indeed should feel fear in dangerous situations. It justified this claim by showing that its contrary—that brave people never are afraid—is incoherent.

In this respect, the story amounts to a philosophical thought experiment, much like the one Socrates presents to Polemarchus.

"Dragons and Giants" also suggested a positive characterization of bravery: persevering in the face of danger. It did this by getting us to reflect on why we thought Frog and Toad acted bravely in their hike up the mountain. Although this doesn't guarantee the truth of this contentions, it does render it plausible as a characteristic of brave actions.

So, it seems clear that "Dragons and Giants" actually does do philosophy. And it does this despite being a very short humorous story accompanied by charming illustrations.

Although "Dragons and Giants" is a pretty special children's story, it is not unique. There are many picture books whose narratives make philosophical problems available to young children and that press them to think philosophically. Unfortunately, this is an area that has not received as much attention from philosophers and picture book scholars as I think it deserves. There is, however, some evidence that philosophers are now paying more attention to picture books as a philosophical resource. A recent anthology entitled *Philosophy in Children's Literature* has essays on Heidegger and *The Velveteen Rabbit*, Nietzsche and *The Rainbow Fish*, *The Giving Tree* and Deep Ecology, and Horton Hears, not a Who, but Badiou. Although this may make you worry that some great children's books are being rendered as unintelligible as some philosophical texts, my suggestion is that these essays show that picture books contain reflections upon the same fundamental issues that have puzzled philosophers. While picture books may not advance our, that is, philosophers and students of philosophy, understanding of issues like authenticity and the appropriate attitude to take toward natural things, they do raise those issues in ways that provide a less sophisticated audience, such as 6-year olds, with access to those issues and arguments about them. My own book, *A Sneetch Is a Sneetch and Other Philosophical Discoveries* presents the philosophical content of a number of picture books without on the whole much reference to obscure philosophical writing.

Our exploration of the philosophy done by "Dragons and Giants" provides another reason for using picture books to teach children philosophy. Because a simple story like this depicts its characters actually engaged in doing philosophy, say by making the distinction between being brave and appearing brave, children are provided with simple examples of what doing philosophy requires. In discussing his own philosophical novels, Lipman called this "modeling." I was critical of him for not explaining how such modeling was supposed to work to get children to understand the nature of philosophical dialogues. The difference is that, in discussing bravery through "Dragons and Giants," children come to see both Frog and Toad as engaged in the very same type of activity as they are. By carefully reflecting on the story, the children are pushed into engaging in the activity of philosophizing in a very natural way, one that is modeled by the interactions between the story's two protagonists.

Notes

1 The musical can be viewed at https://www.youtube.com/watch?v=23HmmQeCxiA.
2 The contrast between bravery, cowardice, and rashness was first articulated by Aristotle in his *Nicomachean Ethics*. Although bravery and cowardice are used in ordinary English, rashness is not as common. I know of no better term for this character trait.
3 The issue of whether contradictions should be rejected or embraced is nearly as old as philosophy itself. Some see Heraclitus as embracing contradiction and Parmenides as rejecting it. There are even contemporary views of logic that see contradictions as unproblematic. See, for example, Graham Priest (2006).

PART III

Issues about Facilitating Picture-Book Philosophy Discussions

7

HOW SOMEONE WHO DOESN'T ALREADY KNOW PHILOSOPHY CAN TEACH IT

When discussing *Where the Wild Things Are*, I relied upon a distinction between two different senses of the word "reality." "Objective reality" referred to actual events taking place in the shared world of spatiotemporal objects, while "subjective reality" referred to things taking place within Max's mind. Such a distinction is one that philosophers often make. This brings to the fore a question that has dogged philosophy for/with children practitioners: how much philosophy does a facilitator of an elementary-school philosophy discussion need to know?

As usual, we find Matthew Lipman staking out a clear but controversial position on this question. He believed that people interested in facilitating philosophy discussions had to have a background in philosophy and, indeed, education in order to be effective. That's why he argued for the necessity of attending training sessions aimed at providing the essentials that a facilitator needs and also produced massive teacher manuals for his books that supply a wealth of background knowledge. He thought that anyone who had attended the training sessions and had the teachers' manuals as guides was in a position to facilitate elementary-school philosophy discussions.

In my earlier book, *Big Ideas for Little Kids: Teaching Philosophy Through Children's Literature*, I asserted that *anyone* could facilitate elementary-school philosophy discussion, even those without a background in philosophy. But I was not saying that a facilitator did not need to have *any* philosophical knowledge in order to facilitate a philosophical discussion. I only claimed that they could find all the information they needed in my book because it presented detailed analyses of a set of picture books I suggested using, including a discussion of the philosophical theses put forward in each picture book.

DOI: 10.4324/9781003257455-10

Because my book also included chapters outlining the methodology that I favored using in philosophical dialogues, I felt justified in saying that anyone who possessed the book could begin facilitating such discussions among elementary-school children. Still, more needs to be said about what knowledge and skills facilitators need in order to be successful in overseeing philosophy discussions. That is the task I set out to accomplish in this chapter.

7.1 Methodological Background

At this point, it will be useful to explore how our elementary-school philosophy discussions are conducted. I generally prefer working with a group of 10–15 students, although it's possible to work with larger or smaller groups as well. They can be from a single grade or from a number of different ones. If the age of the students varies too much, the facilitator will have to be cognizant of the different ages of the participants to make sure that everyone has an equal opportunity to take part in the discussion.

As I have already mentioned a number of times, we begin our session with a read-aloud. This requires that a book has been chosen. There are many ways to do this. The website I created, http://www.teachingchildrenphilosophy.org,[1] has over 300 books on it. For each book, there is a brief summary of the narrative and an introduction to the philosophical issues it raises. There are also lists of suggested questions that can help a facilitator organize their ideas about how to structure a dialogue.

Once the book has been chosen, the facilitator needs to become familiar with it. This entails a number of different things. First, they need to know the plot of the story. This requires reading the book a couple of times. It is helpful to read the book aloud at least once to discover any problematic places there might be. Also, during the readings, they should keep a list of any vocabulary words that might not be familiar to the students. It's a good idea to go over them with the students prior to reading the story aloud to make sure they understand them. It's also important for the facilitator to become familiar with the philosophical issue(s) that they see the book raising and that they expect the children to discuss. This doesn't require reading vast amounts of literature on the issue in question, but only thinking through all the related questions that might arise, perhaps in conjunction with looking on teachingchildrenphilosophy.org which includes a brief introduction to the philosophical issues raised by each of the books is presents.

I suggest making a *concept map*. A concept map is a diagram of all the central concepts that a story raises and the relationships between them. Consider the story that I discussed in Chapter 3, "Cookies." The central concept in that story is will power. This would sit in the central circle of the concept map. As I will explain in a moment, two related concepts are desire and reason. These can be added to the concept map along with some other concepts such as action and inhibition. The result is a diagram that looks like Figure 7.1.

FIGURE 7.1   Concept Map Diagram

The point of making a concept map is to create a simple visual representation of the philosophical concepts that the story employs and the relationships that hold between them. This will help the facilitator as she oversees the children's discussion.

Incidentally, it's a good idea to create a version of the concept map while the children are discussing the book, using the concepts they mention. Whenever a "big idea" surfaces during the discussion, the facilitator can just note this on the concept map. This provides a nice record of how the discussion has progressed and what new ideas have been developed during it. The facilitator can refer to it to explain how the discussion has resulted in a more complex understanding of the central concepts that have been discussed.

The read-aloud itself is fairly simple. With the students sitting in a circle either on a rug or on chairs, the facilitator just reads the book to the students. There are a couple of important pieces of advice about this. First, it's helpful to use "voices" to make the story interesting. A facilitator does not have to be a trained actor to make the story more entertaining by voicing the different characters. When I was working in New Zealand at the Island Bay School, I always voiced the characters when I read to the children. But I was very surprised to discover that the teachers wanted me to voice the characters when reading a story to *them* during a workshop. Adults enjoy a dramatic reading as much as children, I guess.

Showing the pictures in the book to the children is crucial. Clearly, an important element in the appeal of picture books is their illustrations. Children want to see them. So, when the facilitator reads the book, they also need to show the children the images. This is best done by holding the book with the cover toward oneself and then slowly rotating the book to show the picture to all the students in succession. Learning to read upside down helps!

Once the reading is over, it's time for the discussion. We present the students with a short set of guidelines that are necessary for having a philosophy discussion. Some of these guidelines have to do with the culture of the classroom in which a philosophy discussion can take place. We ask the students to treat one another with respect, seeing everyone as having a unique perspective that can make an important contribution to the discussion. And we encourage them to have fun, for philosophical discussions should be enjoyable and not a chore.

The other guidelines have to do with the different "moves" that constitute the "game" of philosophy. I have developed a mnemonic that helps everyone remember them: **SLAW**. Here is what that means:

> **S**ay what you think.
> **L**isten to what others have to say.
> Figure out if you **A**gree or Disagree with what has been said.
> Say **W**hy you think what you do, i.e., give reasons for your beliefs.

As the discussion proceeds, the facilitator can use this list of the allowable moves in a philosophical discussion as a guide in monitoring the discussion. They can even post these in the classroom to have them to refer to during the discussion. The children will soon master them.

The discussion begins when the facilitator asks the students a question. They should have determined in advance which question they want to begin with. After asking the question, it is helpful to give the students a little time to consider their responses unless, as sometimes happens, they are eager to begin talking.

Once a child has responded, the facilitator should generally continue the discussion by asking, "Who agrees or disagrees with what has been said and why?" This reminds the children of what they need to do in a philosophical discussion and opens the floor for anyone to make a comment. It also immediately connects the other students to the one who has made the first comment.

A crucial skill that the facilitator must employ is that of *deep listening*. Over the years, I have come to realize that most of us are terrible listeners. We all want to express our own beliefs and pay much less attention to what others have to say. When taking part in a philosophical discussion, however, all the participants have to listen intently to what everyone else is saying. This holds not only for the students but also for the facilitator. Only if the facilitator listens very carefully to what the children are saying will they be able to guide the discussion appropriately.

Earlier, I mentioned that the dominant view among practitioners of philosophy for children is that the children should set the agenda and that this conflicts with our practice of asking the first question. So, let me admit that I have sometimes let the children decide what topic to discuss. Once, while I was teaching at the Island Bay School, we were going to discuss "The Garden," one of Arnold Lobel's charming Frog and Toad stories.[2] Toad wants to have a garden but gets impatient when the seeds don't sprout immediately. He tries a variety of different inappropriate ways to get the seeds to grow, such as shouting at them or reading to them.

I had anticipated discussing what different types of beings there were in the world and what types of behavior were appropriate for each of them, reflecting on the philosophical mistake Toad had made by treating the seeds as if they could hear him. But one of the girls in the group, Zoe, said that she wanted to discuss patience and impatience. I was surprised but decided to let the discussion proceed in the direction Zoe had suggested. The question that eventually emerged was whether it was always a good thing to be patient. After all, it seems like being impatient is not a good character trait to have, and parents attempt to teach their children to be patient, to acquire that skill.

But what the children said during our dialogue was that there are certain circumstances in which patience is not a good thing. The example they gave was patience in the face of injustice. They pointed out that Martin Luther King, Jr. was not patient in his attempt to confront American racism. Impatience in such circumstances was a good trait to have.

I was pleasantly surprised by the course our discussion took. I had operated with the standard view of impatience as what philosophers call "a vice," that is, a character trait that was morally problematic. The students did a piece of innovative philosophical reasoning when they claimed that, in certain circumstances, impatience can be a virtue. I would not have made that claim myself, but came to see that their view was actually correct. These young philosophers had put forward a very creative view about the morality of patience that contradicts the standard view I had accepted. So, I actually learned something by allowing them to pursue their own interests during our session.

I should add that, when a facilitator lets the students choose the topic to discuss, they need to have enough of a background in philosophy to be able to judge whether or not the discussion is proceeding in a philosophically useful manner. One reason that I start the discussions with a preselected question is that this ensures that the initial question is a philosophical one. It also allows the facilitator to be better prepared.

Because the book modules on teachingchildrenphilosophy.org list many different questions that could be asked in relation to a given text, there is a temptation for the facilitator to treat the question list much like a recipe. When you are cooking, a recipe gives you a series of steps you need to follow to make the dish you want. You can't skip a step without risking ruining the dish.

Philosophical discussions are not like that. Once the children have begun to discuss a topic, the facilitator should listen to what they say, guiding the discussion in philosophically useful ways. But just posing another question from the list tends to derail the discussion rather than fostering it. Introducing new topics needs to be done judiciously and only when it's clear that a previous topic has been thoroughly discussed.

It is worth pointing out that there is a set of strategies that facilitators can turn to when they want to move the conversation forward. For example, when a student says something that is not particularly clear to the facilitator, they might intervene by asking the student to *explain* what they meant by their comment. This will ensure that the discussion proceeds with a clear understanding of the comment.

A facilitator might also attempt to get more clarification by asking a student who has made a comment to give an *example* of the phenomenon that they have pointed to. If a student says, for example, that people are inherently self-ish even when they appear not to be, it would be useful to ask for an example to help the other students understand what that student was thinking.

These are just two examples of the sorts of interventions that a facilitator can use to assist the students during their philosophical conversations.[3] They are simply ways to make sure that the dialogue proceeds on the basis of a shared understanding of what has been said. Throughout the discussion, the facilitator should remember that the best strategy is to keep asking the class what they think—do they agree or disagree?—about what has been said.

When a facilitator is successful in getting a group of children to discuss a philosophical topic in accordance with the guidelines we have suggested, the classroom becomes what practitioners call "a community of philosophical inquiry." The classroom will have become a *community* in the sense that the individual children have come to see themselves and their classmates not as separate individuals but as members of a collectivity, a group this is united by a common purpose. What unites the students is their commitment to engaging in a philosophical discussion.

The term *inquiry* derives from the work of the American pragmatist philosopher Charles Sanders Peirce who used the term to characterize the nature of scientific practice. For Peirce, "inquiry" is a process by means of which scientists attempt to discover the secrets of nature. To inquire is to seek to gain knowledge about some object or topic. The students who engage in elementary-school philosophy discussions create a community out of their classroom in so far as they are all united in their attempt to conduct an inquiry into an issue.

This, in rough outline, is what a philosophical discussion for elementary school students looks like. I like to say that its goal is teaching the children how to *think for themselves together.* This slightly paradoxical phrasing indicates that the children are able to accomplish more working together than they can individually. But when they do so, they don't accept the results of their discussion, their inquiry, because others accept it. The ultimate tribunal is their own acceptance of a view on the basis of the arguments that have been given to support it.

I began this chapter with the question, "How much philosophy does a good facilitator of elementary-school philosophical discussions need to know?" What has emerged is that there is no general answer to this question. Because there are many resources that a facilitator can use in preparing to lead a philosophical discussion, they do not need to have a huge amount of pre-existing philosophical knowledge to draw on. On the other hand, if they choose to let the children discuss issues of their choosing, a broad background in philosophy will be helpful in assisting them in making sure the discussion is proceeding in a philosophically satisfying manner.

In general, we should bear in mind that facilitators will gain philosophical knowledge as a result of facilitating philosophical discussions. The amount of knowledge a facilitator possesses will constantly be changing, for their engagement with philosophy will result in their acquiring more insight and understanding of philosophical issues. I pointed out, for example, that my own view of patience changed as a result of a discussion among students at the Island Bay School.

Maybe the appropriate conclusion to draw is that facilitators do not have to *begin* with a large amount of philosophical knowledge, but that they will benefit from the acquisition of such knowledge for it will help them become skilled facilitators for a classroom community of inquiry. And they do need to have a sense of what a philosophical statement is like in order to assist the children in taking part in a philosophical conversation.

7.2 The Important Book

I am now going to illustrate the claims I have made about the philosophical knowledge necessary for facilitating an elementary-school philosophy discussion with reference to Margaret Wise Brown's *The Important Book* (1949). Wise Brown wrote a number of well-known children's book, most notably *Good Night Moon* (1947). She was also a student of philosophy, having studied with John Dewey.

The Important Book consists of ten spreads each of which contains images of an object that the text concerns and a verbal description of things that are true about that object. Each spread focuses on a single object: a spoon, a daisy, rain, grass, snow, an apple, the wind, the sky (yes, it's blue), a shoe, and you. The verbal description in each spread has the same form. First, it says that one property of the object is "the important thing" about the object. Then, a number of other properties that the object possesses are listed. Finally, the statement about the important thing about the object is repeated.

Let's consider the first spread about a spoon. Here is what the book says:

> The important thing about a spoon is that you eat with it.
> It's like a little shovel,
> You hold it in your hand,
> You can put it in your mouth,
> It isn't flat,
> It's hollow,
> And it spoons things up.
> But the important thing about a spoon is that you eat with it.

It is obvious that there are many problems with the statements the book makes about a spoon. First, if what the book calls "the important thing" about an object is supposed to distinguish it from all other types of things, then the book's claim about a spoon is simply not true. While you do eat with a spoon, you also eat with forks and knives, for example. So, the property of being something you eat with does not adequately distinguish a spoon from all other things. At best, it is, in philosophical parlance, a necessary but not sufficient condition of something being a spoon.

Next, consider the other properties of a spoon that are mentioned. Let's just look at the statement that you can put it in your mouth. While it is true for teaspoons and soup spoons, it's not true for serving spoons which are too big to fit comfortably into a person's mouth, especially a child's. And there are pictures of a spoon in magazines, but they cannot be put in a person's mouth. So, this property is not one that holds of all spoons, but only some of them.

Given what I have just said, it's clear that a philosophical discussion about what the book says about spoons is easy to initiate. It would likely result in the participants agreeing that the property of being something that you eat with is a necessary but not sufficient condition of something being a spoon, though we would never use those terms with the children. In addition, the book's claim that spoons fit into a person's mouth would likely be rejected as not holding for spoons in general but only certain subsets of them.

Such a discussion could take place for virtually all of the other objects discussed by the book, from a daisy to "you." But these discussions are not yet philosophical since they focus only on the properties of different types of objects. This doesn't mean that a philosophical discussion cannot be based upon *The Important Book*, but only that it's not obvious what topic(s) it would focus upon. This indicates why a facilitator needs to have a sense of what makes a discussion philosophical.

In order to see how *The Important Book* could be the basis of an interesting philosophical discussion, I will need to discuss some philosophy, specifically Aristotle's theory of *essentialism*. This is because I take *The Important Book* to be attempting to demonstrate the validity of Aristotle's theory. (Alternatively, one could take the book to be criticizing Aristotle's account, but I will ignore that possibility here.)

According to Aristotle, we need to distinguish between two types of properties that things possess. *Properties* are simply characteristics that an object or thing has. It is a property of fire that it burns things, just as it is a property of water that it extinguishes fires. Aristotle claimed that many properties that a thing possesses can change without the thing ceasing to be the type of thing that it is. A fire can spread, i.e., cover a larger area than it initially did, without it ceasing to be a fire, for example. Or a man can go bald without ceasing to be the person that he was. Such properties Aristotle called *accidents* to indicate that they can change without altering a thing's nature.

But there is one property that a thing possesses—its *essence* or *essential property* according to Aristotle—that cannot change without the thing ceasing to be the type of thing that it is. Consider a soup spoon. It's at least plausible to say that its essential property is being something with which a person can eat soup.

Say that something caused it to no longer be rigid but to be "droopy" so that any time you tried to scoop up some soup it would just bend and let the soup run out of it. It's plausible to say that it would no longer be a soup spoon or, at least, that it was no longer capable of functioning as one. It's essence, Aristotle would say, had changed.

In order to have a philosophical discussion of *The Important Book*, the facilitator needs to realize that the book illustrates Aristotle's theory of essentialism by claiming that each of the objects it discusses has an "important" or "essential" property along with a number of others, its "accidents." The idea is *not* to tell the students that this is what the book is doing, but to use *our* understanding of what the book is about to generate questions that address the adequacy of Aristotle's theory.

Once we understand that the subject of *The Important Book* is the theory of essentialism, we can see how to transform a discussion about the claims the book makes about various objects into a genuinely philosophical one. After discussing the adequacy of some of the claims made by the book, a facilitator can ask the students whether they agree with the book that every object has one property—one thing that is true of it—that is "the important thing" about that object. (Notice that this does not require introducing *them* to Aristotle's terminology and certainly not explaining his theory to them. Instead, the book's language of "important things" is retained during the discussion.)

When I have asked children this question, some of them accept the claim that there is one important thing about each object. But they face the problem of dealing with all the false statements about "important things" that the book makes. Other students deny that objects have important features other than "all of them." Their idea is that every property that an object possesses is as important to its nature as any other. Only the entire ensemble of properties is the "important thing" about that object.

The children who take part in this discussion are reflecting on an important principle in *metaphysics*. Metaphysics is the branch of philosophy that reflects on the ultimate structure of that which exists. The claim that every object has an important or essential property is a metaphysical one. So, in discussing *The Important Book*, children get introduced to metaphysics. Once again, there is no need to *tell them* that they have been having a discussion about a metaphysical issue, though they might enjoy learning what a complicated philosophical term means.

It is worth pointing out that a discussion like the one I have outlined here will enhance children's wonder about the world. They will see that the concepts that we use as if they were completely unproblematic in the course of living our lives are much more puzzling and intricate than we ordinarily think. This will demonstrate to them that reality is endlessly fascinating and a suitable subject for philosophical discussions.

The important thing [sic.] for us to realize about philosophical discussions is that they have to move beyond a consideration of merely factual or empirical claims. When children are critical of *The Important Book* for claiming that the important thing about a spoon is that you eat with it, they are not yet discussing a philosophical thesis, but an empirical one about the nature of spoons. But when the discussion moves to considering the thesis that every object has "an important thing" about it, the discussion has moved into the realm of philosophy. This is because the thesis they are discussing is no longer an empirical one, but a theoretical claim about the nature of objects, the domain, as I have just said, of metaphysics.

Of course, the discussion does not have to ask *that* particular question in order to become philosophical. Another topic that is equally philosophical is whether an object's structure or function is more important. When the book states that the important thing about a spoon is that you eat with it, it is treating the spoon's *function* as fundamental to its nature.

If the discussion moves onto the question of whether objects are most fundamentally characterized by their function or their structure, once again there is room for disagreement and a philosophical discussion. Despite the book's claim about the function of a spoon, one could argue that their *structure* is equally fundamental. It might be pointed out that a spoon has to be "hollow," a structural property mentioned by the book, in order for it to fulfill its function of allowing a person to eat (liquids) with it.

If we reflect on the questions that turn a discussion of an empirical question—What is the important thing about a spoon?—into a philosophical one—Is there one and only one important thing that is true of every object?—we can see that the questions are guided by the facilitator's knowledge of what makes a question philosophical. That's why they ask whether objects only have one important thing that is true about them or whether objects are more fundamentally determined by their structure or their function. By doing so, they have, so to speak, moved the discussion "up a level," from the empirical to the philosophical.

For this reason, it becomes evident that, without some knowledge of the philosophical ideas that a book mobilizes, it would be hard for a teacher, parent, or other adult to come up with the questions that can transform an empirical discussion into a philosophical one. At the same time, we need to realize that it doesn't take a tremendous amount of philosophical knowledge to be proficient in guiding a discussion of a picture book like *The Important Book*. That is why I was able to provide an outline of such knowledge in my discussion of the books in *Big Ideas for Little Kids*. But it does mean that anyone interested in facilitating a philosophical discussion with and among elementary-school children ought to have some knowledge of the philosophical area she expects the children to discuss.

But even when a facilitator has a good background in the philosophical topic that is being discussed, they need to refrain from explaining the issues to the children, as tempting as that might be. They need to remain true to the guiding principle of p4/wc: the children are to engage in the activity of philosophizing rather than learning what philosophers have thought about an issue. Only in this way will children have their concerns addressed through philosophical dialogues with their peers.

7.3 Conclusion

This chapter has focused on the question of whether facilitators of elementary-school philosophy discussions need to possess knowledge of the topics that arise in the discussions that they monitor. I have argued that in order to get the children to actually discuss philosophy, a facilitator would do well to have some prior knowledge of philosophy. The reason for this is that a facilitator often has to transform a discussion of an empirical issue into one about a philosophical one. This requires that the discussion move to a more abstract level than it initially had, as we have seen in the case of *The Important Book*.

But even when the need for some prior knowledge is admitted, I don't think that a facilitator needs special training to be able to introduce philosophical discussions into an elementary-school classroom, useful as such training can be. As they acquire more experience facilitating such conversations, facilitators will also come to possess not just more knowledge about philosophical topics, but a more adequate sense of what philosophy as a discipline is. This more general knowledge will let them recognize when a student has made a philosophically significant contribution and when not. Such knowledge acquisition can come about organically, as the facilitator finds themself engaging children in philosophical discussions with increasing frequency.

Notes

1 The website is now run by the Prindle Ethics Institute at DePauw University. The actual URL is https://www.prindleinstitute.org/teaching-children-philosophy/.
2 Arnold Lobel's Frog and Toad stories keep coming up as examples. One reason why I like using these stories is their brevity. It's easy to read the book in a few minutes, giving the group more time to discuss the philosophical issues than when a longer picture book like *Where the Wild Things Are* is used.
3 In his 2019 book, Peter Worley compiles many such questions.

8

USING PICTURE BOOKS TO DISCUSS RACIAL ISSUES

Recently, there has been a heated debate among practitioners of philosophy for children about whether picture books can be used as the basis for philosophical discussions of complex social issues. The topic that the debate has focused upon is racism and whether some of the books used to introduce children to this complex issue actually are adequate to the task. Taking off from suggestions about using books like David McKee's *Tusk Tusk* (1978) to get students thinking about race and racism, the debate has raised the issue of whether using picture books can result in children acquiring an adequate understanding of racism, or whether these books simply perpetuate misleading accounts of racism's nature.

While the critics of using picture books to teach racism have raised important issues, they have failed to look into the wide variety of ways that picture books have incorporated issues of race and racism into their narratives and illustrations. I will argue that there are certain contemporary picture books that can be used successfully to teach race and racism to young children, so that the concern that picture books inherently present a misleading picture of complex social issues is simply misguided.

More broadly considered, this debate provides a good opportunity to consider the question of what criteria should be used to choose books to discuss with children. The choice of books will affect the types of issues that get discussed in philosophy classes, so it's important to have a clear understanding of the factors that should determine what books to use.

The current debate about picture books was inspired by Darren Chetty, who, in a 2014 article, criticizes the use of certain picture books to teach children about race and racism. He asserts that the a-historical and a-contextual nature of such picture books serves to reinforce rather than criticize racist

DOI: 10.4324/9781003257455-11

ideas such as White Supremacy. As a result, he is not sanguine about the possibility of using picture books to discuss race with young children.

As background to his criticism, Chetty goes over the basic assumptions of Critical Race Theory and, in particular, Charles Mills' theory of a racial contract. Among the important ideas he mentions is white people's blindness to their own racial characteristics. Whereas black adults and children generally characterize their own identities in racial terms, whites do not, taking whiteness to be both invisible and normative.

One aim of Critical Race Theory is to make whiteness more visible. This requires understanding the historical dimensions of racism, that is, the historical process whereby the economic and social inequalities of today's society came into being through a racialized society that explicitly justified the oppression of non-white people.

Against the background of this conception of racism's nature and history, Chetty turns to the use of picture books to teach children about racism. In particular, he looks at two books by David McKee—*Elmer* (1989) and *Tusk Tusk* (1978)—that have been recommended by philosophy for children practitioners as good books for teaching children about racism. Although Chetty does express doubts as to whether these books are actually about racism, he ignores those doubts and goes on to discuss them as if they did address this issue. This is a serious error that causes Chetty to hold an erroneous position concerning the usefulness of picture books for discussing serious social issues.

8.1 Elmer

Let's begin with *Elmer*. *Elmer* is the story of an elephant whose skin is not the normal grey color of the skin of all the other elephants. Instead, Elmer's skin resembles a patchwork quilt. Upset by his difference from all the other elephants, Elmer rolls in some berries until his skin appears to be the same color as that of the other elephants. When he returns to the herd, the other elephants don't recognize him, but they seem more serious than usual. Elmer cracks a jokes and all the elephants laugh. Only when a rainstorm destroys his camouflage, is Elmer outed. Once they realize Elmer's feelings, the other elephants decide to have a yearly celebration in which they paint themselves to look like Elmer and he gets to display his "normal" skin that has been colored by the berries.

Although I understand the temptation to interpret the book about skin color as the basis for differentiating racial groups, I think this misinterprets the book's narrative.[1] The book never specifies anything about how the difference between Elmer's skin color and that of the other elephants is to be interpreted. All the narrative presents us with an elephant who is different from all the other elephants and wants to erase that difference. Elmer is an elephant who desires to be like all the other elephants and, in his case, this means having the color skin that they all share.

If we reflect upon how this theme—that difference from the other members of one's group is problematic—acquires a philosophical register, we run into a theme that has been discussed by the Existentialists, namely that of *authenticity*. For the Existentialists, most people desire to be like one another, to conform to the norms that "everyone" accepts. To such people—referred to by Existentialists as the herd, the They, the masses—being different is a real problem that the most people seek to overcome by assimilating themselves to the standards represented by others.

These people's view of the world is not, according to the Existentialists, the correct one. The norm that should govern our conduct is not one that asks us to conform to the values and choices of others, but rather that of becoming *an individual*, that is, someone who values their own unique nature that differentiates them from the rest of the people in the herd.

This is the lesson that Elmer learns from his attempt to pass as a "normal" elephant. He sees that the other members of his herd do not reject him for having a different colored skin but rather celebrate his uniqueness. This is the reason for their yearly celebration in which they dress up like Elmer.

Confirmation of my interpretation of *Elmer* comes from the fact that the issue of difference is one that has been addressed by other picture books even though those books view the topic differently. Consider, for example, Marcus Fister's *The Rainbow Fish* (1992). Here is how the book is described on its website (https:rainbowfish.us):

> Rainbow Fish is the most beautiful fish in the ocean, his scales shimmering the colors of the rainbow. When the other fish see him they want shimmering scales too, but Rainbow Fish keeps the beautiful scales to himself. His choice not to share soon makes Rainbow Fish a lonely fish. He discovers, in the end, that in sharing his scales, not only does he bring a smile to others, but he feels happy as well.

The appeal of this book, on this interpretation, is its message that sharing is a good thing for those who receive a gift but also for those who give it. In this way, the book aims to enhance children's ethical formation by getting them to acknowledge the benefits of sharing.

For the Existentialist, however, the book's message is troubling. As Claudia Mills has argued (2012), the book celebrates the very conformity that philosophers in the Existential tradition have criticized. (Mills uses Nietzsche's notion of *slave morality* to ground her claims.) So, rather than endorsing the book's message about the benefits of giving, Mills is critical of the book for supporting conformity and undermining children's desire to become individuals.

Incidentally, Mills' interpretation of *The Rainbow Fish* is a good example of a "reading against the grain," a literary strategy endorsed by Chetty.[2] The distinction between reading "with the grain" and "against the grain" is clearly made by David Bartholomae and Anthony Petrosky in their book *Ways of Reading*. In the Preface to the book, they say: "To read generously, to work within someone else's system, to see your world in someone else's terms – this we call 'reading with the grain'." They also describe what it is to "read against the grain": "to read critically, to turn back, for example, *against* an author's project, to ask questions they believe might come as a surprise, to look for the limits of their vision, to provide alternate readings of the examples, to find examples that challenge their arguments – to engage the author, in other words, in dialogue" (Bartholomae and Petrosky, 2019).

It's clear that Mills' reading is one that proceeds "against the grain." This is because she is using Nietzsche's distinction between slave and master moralities as a means of critiquing the book's valorization of the rainbow fish's decision to share his scales with the other fish, a decision that undermines his individuality and distinctiveness.

Elmer, on the other hand, celebrates the very individuality that *The Rainbow Fish* criticizes. My interpretation of *Elmer* is supported by the fact that *The Rainbow Fish* addresses that very issue albeit with a different take on it. The fact that picture books can disagree about philosophical issues such as the importance of individuality is one reason that they are so useful for philosophy discussions.

I want to point out that the idea of reading against the grain is not a helpful way to think about philosophy discussions. A philosophy discussion cannot be conceptualized as either with or against the grain. This is because philosophy requires a movement away from the empirical toward abstraction. Rather than asking what the creator of a picture book might have had in mind, as one does when one reads "with the grain," or what an author might not have been able to acknowledge about the text, which is the basic question of readings "against the grain," a philosophical discussion focuses on the *ideas* or *concepts* at issue in a book or discussion, asking the participants to reflect upon them. The aim is to explore the meaning of concepts like that of an object's essential property, not to construct an interpretation of the text that is either for or against the grain.

In this respect, the philosophy discussions we have with children about picture books resemble Socrates' practice as depicted in the early dialogues of Plato, for Socrates is always questioning his discussion partners about the meaning of an important concept. When Socrates encounters Euthyphro on the steps of the courthouse where he will soon be tried, for example, he asks him to explain what holiness or piety is, since that's the basis upon which Euthyphro is taking his own father to court. Socrates is less concerned with Euthyphro's motivation for prosecuting his own father than with his understanding of the concept that forms the basis for his action.

8.2 Tusk Tusk

Another book by McKee, *Tusk Tusk*, has also been interpreted as a book about racism, once again mistakenly in my opinion. The story focuses on two groups of elephants that are distinguished by the color of their skin. These black and white elephants hate one another and embark on a fight to the death.[3] They eventually kill each other off. The grey grandchildren of the original elephants return from the forest to which their parents had fled during the initial round of fighting, only to find themselves becoming hostile to elephants who do not have the same size ears as they do. The book's ambiguous ending leaves the reader with the impression that ear size will soon be used to justify another life-and-death struggle among the younger elephants.

The question we need to ask is whether this story is actually about race and racism. Chetty points out that there are many disanalogies between the manner in which racism functions in reality and the way the story presents the hostility between the different groups of elephants (Chetty, 2014, pp. 21–22). The most significant are: (1) the book presents no reason why the elephants are hostile to one another and (2) one group of elephants is not presented as dominating the other. Chetty takes this to show that the book embraces a fundamentally flawed view of racism, for he takes the two characteristics lacking in the book to be essential to racism.

Chetty focuses on this book because Haynes and Murris (2012, p. 115) suggested that it was a good book to use to discuss racism, particularly in the context of post-Apartheid South Africa. He argues that the book cannot support this usage since it fails to incorporate an adequate conception of racism. Among the features of racism that he believes they ignore are: (1) that racism functions to justify the oppression of one group by another and (2) that racism arises in specific social contexts. He is critical of Haynes and Murris' championing of the book's presentation of racism (if that is what the book is about) for its very abstract and analytical presentation of the issue. While they see this abstractness as central to the book's usefulness for philosophy, Chetty thinks that very abstractness is the result of the book's failure to address the structural nature of racism.

Murris responds to Chetty's critique by reasserting the validity of using books that do not have clear social and cultural contexts.

> I argue…that it is indeed the abstractness (independence of history) of the concepts embedded in such picture books that connect with children's own ideas and interests and therefore challenges adult-centered ontology and epistemology. Enquiries *with* children about the meaning of abstract concepts make it possible for adults to hear young children's metaphorical, imaginative, and philosophical contributions to the pool of knowledge.
>
> (*Murris, 2015, p. 60*)

Murris is critical of Chetty for assuming that he knows what the appropriate theory of racism is and attempting to get children to come to accept it. A discussion shaped by an adult's conception of what the outcome should be fails to grant children the autonomy that is the proper goal of philosophical discussions, according to Murris. The very abstractness of a book like *Tusk Tusk* allows children to develop their own ideas in a manner that adds to our knowledge of racism, she claims.

The question of how much "steering" of the discussion is appropriate to elementary-school philosophy is a vexed one. In Chapter 2, I argued that it is perfectly acceptable to begin such discussions by asking the children a question about the book that has been read to them, despite the dominant view among many philosophy for children practitioners that the children should set the agenda for the discussion. Asking the initial question does not take away children's ownership of the course of the discussion they are participating in and can even indicate the interest the facilitator has in *their*, i.e., the children's, beliefs.

What happens if we decide that *Tusk Tusk* is not actually about race? I maintain that this is the case despite Haynes and Murris' (2012) endorsement of the book as a good one to use in philosophical discussions of the nature of racism.[4] Although the book's use of skin color as a marker that undergirds the elephants' hostility to those who are different from them does suggest that the book is about racism, for skin color is certainly one important difference at the basis for racial discrimination, the book's presentation of skin color, as Chetty notes, does not fit our understanding of its role in racist ideology.

If the book is not about racism, what is it about? I see it as a fable—Chetty uses this term quite appropriately to characterize the book's lack of social specificity in describing the situation of the elephants—about the irrationality of war. On such an interpretation, the book presents war as taking place on the basis of a completely superficial characteristic—skin color in this instance—that distinguishes one group from another. Think about, for example, the hostility between the Germans and the French. In the twentieth century, this led to mass killings in two World Wars. But there is no reasonable way to explain why being French, say, makes one an enemy of and inferior to Germans or vice versa.

The irrationality of using a superficial characteristic as the basis for war is emphasized when the grandchildren of the original elephants begin to see having a different ear size as a reason to hate a group of other elephants. The palpable absurdity of starting to hate and eventually kill those with a different ear size grounds the book's case for the absurdity of war.

How adequate is the book's take on war's absurdity? It certainly is a very abstract account that does not include any more specific social factors that explain the origin of a war. Any explanation of an actual war, such as the Second World War, requires more than an acknowledgment of the irrational hostility between, say, the French and the Germans even if that hostility is a factor, say by discussing the impact of the Treaty of Versailles. Nonetheless, I think that the book can engender an interesting discussion of the basis for war, even if it does not by itself present an adequate account of why wars take place.

8.3 Williams on Picture Books

In order to take account of Chetty's criticisms of the failure of philosophy for children practitioners to develop an adequate method for discussing racism, Steve Williams takes up the idea mentioned by Chetty of "reading against the text" (Williams, 2020). Here is Williams' summary of Chetty's critique and his own proposal that attempts to honor it:

> Chetty's argument seems to be that it is not likely that children's picture books alone, particularly in the form of fables, can present this level of complexity and "blending." I take him to imply that other kinds of picture books and alternative materials—or combination of materials—might be more suitable for exploring complex social issues with historical dimensions.
>
> (*Williams, 2020, p. 7*)

Williams goes on to critique Murris' recent position on picture books. Murris argues that picture books are an ideal way to introduce children to philosophy: "picture books are perfect provocations for philosophical questioning" (Murris, 2016b, p. 208). Williams points out that Murris has not taken account of Chetty's argument, but merely opposed her own endorsement of the abstract nature of some picture books to Chetty's criticisms of them. She seems to want to avoid contextualizing stories in time, culture, and place, and make the locus of philosophical activity the matrix of "text, educator, and learners." (Williams, 2020, p. 11).

In attempting to acknowledge the validity of Chetty's critique that picture books either simplify major complex issues and ideas or de-historicize them, Williams suggests that books such as *Tusk Tusk* can be used so long as they are supplemented with other materials from non-fiction as well as fictionalized accounts set in specific historical and social contexts. He puts forward Jaqueline Woodson's 2001 picture book, *The Other Side*, as an example of a book that, as opposed to *Tusk Tusk*, is located in a very specific social context, namely the deep South during segregation. The two girls in the story overcome the "rules" set by the adults in a way that suggests that children are not bound by the same racist norms that their parents acknowledge. Williams continues by offering concrete suggestions on how a facilitator might read against the grain by inviting evaluative judgements, questioning implied and imbedded concepts, and using carefully constructed reflective dialogues, both within and without the group setting.

It is true that *The Other Side* is not an abstract fable like *Tusk Tusk*, for it has a specific social and historical location, viz. the American South in the 1950s or 1960s. Its message is that the young girls do not necessarily accept the social norms about race that dominated the South at that time. But this does not provide anything like the view of racism that Chetty takes from Mills, for it does not address the reasons for racism's existence nor the way in which it negatively impacts the lives of people of color.

So, if Williams' proposal does not satisfy Chetty's demand that philosophy for children needs a more adequate way of addressing issues of racism and social oppression more generally, can anything be done to justify using picture books to discuss this fraught issue? I think it can be and proceed to do so in the next section of this chapter.

8.4 Addressing Race through Picture Books

Let's return to the question of choosing the picture books to use in philosophy classes. One objectionable feature of many picture books, at least when looked at historically, is that they tend to feature white characters. Although *Alice's Adventures in Wonderland* does not specify the race of its protagonist, John Tenniel's charming drawings depict Alice as a blonde white girl. Could this cause non-white children to fail to identify with Alice in the same way that white children do when they see that she looks like them?

This problem besets philosophical novels as well as picture books. Murris (2016a) claims that, even though Lipman's philosophical novels make no reference to the race of the characters and only minimal reference to their gender, children might not identify with the characters because they are not presented in a realistic manner but rather are depicted as mini-philosophers.[5] She fails to point out the related problem stemming from the use of standard English in Lipman's books: it makes the children sound very different than the voices of, say, African-American children.

One of the salutary developments among recent picture books is the increasing number of books written by non-white authors featuring non-white protagonists. Not only are these non-white characters depicted in the books' illustrations, but they speak the vernacular in the way that young children do. This means that children from those groups will see and hear characters who look and speak like they do. As a result, picture books can support non-white children by presenting their lives as equally significant to that of their white peers.

To see this, consider Matt de la Peña's (2015) book, *Last Stop on Market Street*. The book concerning a young black boy and his grandmother taking a bus after church and traveling through the city. CJ has various complaints to make to his Nana about having to travel on the bus with her. Each time, she has a response that helps CJ feel better about what he is doing. When they finally get to the shelter to distribute food, CJ finds himself glad to have accompanied his Nana on their trip.

Despite having two black characters as its protagonists, *Last Stop on Market Street* does not discuss race or racism directly. But this does not mean that it can't play an important role in alleviating some of the problems associated with using picture books to discuss racism. Because the two protagonists are black, African-American children can identify with them. The context for the story is also one that makes sense to such children. A book like this can help them feel that their lives are as significant as those of their white classmates.

In addition, there are other recently written picture books that provide the context for an appropriate elementary-school discussion of race and racism. The books employ very different strategies, but each addresses racial issues in a manner that does not obscure the systematic nature of racial discrimination and oppression.

Both of the books I mention in this context have a quite different structure from the ones that have been cited in the discussion of this issue so far. These books deal with the existence of racism in the real world albeit in different ways. Marianne Celano et al.'s (2019) picture book, *Something Happened in Our Town: A Child's Story About Racial Injustice*, is a book about the shooting of a black man by a white policeman, a problem that has attracted a huge amount of attention as a result of the Black Lives Matter Movement. The book shows discussions taking place about the shooting in both a black and a white family. The two families raise concerns about the shooting that are appropriate to their own situations. In the final part, John and Emma, the two young children in those families, make friends with Omad, a new boy in their school who comes from a foreign country and can't speak English well, showing that they have learned an important lesson about justice and race from their families' discussions of police shootings.

Clearly, this picture book takes an important political issue—the killing of black men by police—and presents it in a way that young children can understand. By having both a black and a white family react to a police killing in different but related ways, the book attempts to have all students see the issue as one that affects their families. Children who have not had the opportunity to discuss such killings with their families will learn a great deal by seeing how the two children learn from their families' discussions.

One feature of the book that I find particularly praiseworthy is the authors' attempt to apply the idea of justice, first raised in the context of police killings, to the lives of the two young children at school. The children are shown taking the lessons they learned from discussing the killing of a black man and applying it to their own lives at school when a young Arab boy is treated unfairly. They now see injustice as something that affects their lives and realize they have the ability to do something about it.

It might seem difficult to have a discussion about this book in a classroom. For one thing, young children are not in a position to come up with realistic policy proposals for dealing with police violence. In addition, this doesn't seem like an ethical issue that has two sides to it. The killings are generally unjustified although there are explanations for their prevalence. This makes it hard to see how a philosophy discussion about police killings of black men could take place in an elementary-school classroom.

Recalling my claim that philosophy discussions revolve around important concepts that are presented in a picture book, we can see a way to use this book to discuss race and racism. One suggestion is to focus on the final incident in the story—John and Emma's sticking up for Omad—for this will allow a genuine philosophical discussion about justice to take place. For example, a facilitator could pose the question of whether not choosing Omad to be on one of the sports teams is unfair and why that might be so. Eventually, the discussion could move onto the notion of fairness or justice itself, in which the children have the opportunity to say what they think makes an action fair or unfair. In this way, they will be participating in a genuine philosophical discussion about a difficult subject.

There are other parts of the story that can also be used. For example, you could ask what the fact that Emma's family had owned slaves in the past means in terms of contemporary policy. The issue of reparations for past wrongs is an important one and could be raised in the context of this book.

My next example of a book that allows for a discussion of race and racism is a very different type of picture book. It presents an actual historical occurrence that is not widely known about. *Separate is Never Equal: Sylvia Mendez and Her Family's Fight for Desegregation* is Duncan Tonatiuh's (2014) book that tells the story of the Mendez family's fight to allow their children to attend the white school near their home rather than the Mexican school to which the district assigned them. It is an inspiring story that culminates in two court cases that established the right to all children to attend the same public schools in California, an important decision that was a forerunner to the more famous case of *Brown vs. the Board of Education* in which the Supreme Court struck down the idea of separate but equal that had been the rule of the land since Reconstruction.

The first thing to say about *Separate is Never Equal* is that it tells a story that has not generally been part of our nation's historical memory. By recovering this history and presenting it in a way that young children can understand, the book provides an important supplement to the way in which America's racist past is understood. The story of the Mendez's fight against segregated schools is one that should be more widely known and this book is part of an effort to publicize the fight and, hence, to give more recognition to the presence of anti-Mexican racism in the United States.

The clearest issue that the book raises and that can form the subject matter for a philosophical dialogue is raised by the book's title: *Separate but Never Equal*. A good place to start a discussion is by asking the children if it ever can be just to have "separate but equal" facilities for two groups of people. If the children don't respond, one fairly obvious place to begin the discussion is by asking about restrooms, a topic I have found children have a significant interest in. Although segregating restrooms by race is generally recognized as unjust—of course, it makes sense to ask why this is so if it comes up—having separate bathrooms for men and women has not always been seen as a social justice issue. Access to bathrooms for transgendered people, though, has been a fraught issue, so discussing segregated bathrooms is a good way to refine children's understanding of what makes a policy or institution just or unjust.

Something Happened in Our Town and *Separate is Never Equal* are two picture books that can be used successfully to discuss race and racism with young children. Both of them feature real historical events—police murder of black men and striking down segregated schools—in a way that helps young children understand them. Because their stories are situated in the real world of racist practices and institutions, these books do not suffer from the problems Chetty attributes to picture books that present "fables" for children to read. As such, they show that picture books can be used to teach about racism so long as they are chosen carefully and with appropriate criteria in mind.

8.5 Conclusion

In this chapter, I have considered a debate among philosophy for children practitioners about using picture books to teach difficult issues such as racism. The debate is useful because it forces us to pay attention to the question of specifying criteria for choosing picture books to use to discuss such issues. We have seen that care has to be taken in basing a discussion of race and racism on picture books that are more fables than realistic accounts of social issues.

What has emerged is that there are certain picture books that can be the basis for such difficult discussions, but they need to be chosen carefully. I have briefly indicated why three recent picture books can function as the basis for philosophical discussions of race. My endorsement of picture books as allowing for successful discussions of difficult issues comes with the *caveat* that the books have to be chosen with care so that inappropriate conceptions of race and racism will not be supported.

Since my discussion has focused exclusively on teaching race as a result of the recent controversy about that issue, it is worthwhile to emphasize the generality of my proposed solution to the problem of teaching difficult topics using picture books. The manner in which I have addressed this issue in regard to race can easily be generalized.

When attempting to have a dialogue about a difficult social issue it is crucial to exercise care in choosing the picture book that will serve as the prompt for the discussion. Perhaps surprisingly, it often turns out to be difficult to determine what the philosophical concern a picture book addresses. As a result, inappropriate picture books have been suggested as appropriate for a discussion of a difficult topic, as we saw was the case with *Elmer* and *Tusk Tusk*.

For a discussion of a difficult topic to result in an appropriate understanding of the issue, the picture book needs to be chosen carefully. In the case of race, I suggested that two books that focus on actual occurrences are more appropriate than some others. This is because these books deal with real events that children ought to know more about. As I pointed out, it is relatively easy to find ways to use these books to stimulate philosophical dialogues.

Earlier, I mentioned another difficult topic for picture-book-based discussions: death. In that case, the book that I suggested using, *The Dead Bird*, did not concern an historical occurrence. Instead, it used a simple fictional scenario—a group of children discovering a dead bird—to raise the question of what happens to creatures when they die. I suggested that, because the book presented death in a way that both related to children and yet was sufficiently distanced that they would not be freaked out by it, it was a good way to introduce students to that difficult topic.

Another, more recent, picture book dealing with death is Jessica Bagley's 2005 *Boats for Papa*. The story focuses on a young beaver, Buckley, and his mama. Buckley loves to build model boats and does so painstakingly. He sends the boats he has made out to sea with a note, "For Papa." When he discovers that his mother has rescued all the boats after that have washed back ashore, Buckley sends out his next creation with the message, "For Mama."

Boats for Papa can be used to discuss how people cope with the death of a loved one, especially a parent. Without making an explicit statement, the book suggests that mourning the loss of a loved one is a process that needs to be undergone. A good place to begin a discussion of the book would be with this question: "Why do you think Buckley isn't angry with his mama for saving all of his boats?"

There is no general recipe that I can put forward that will specify the best picture books to use to discuss a difficult topic. The examples I have given adopt very different strategies for choosing books. In one case, I argued that the books needed to reflect actual events; in the other, the books were more abstract and ahistorical. The fact that each of these strategies can be used in appropriate circumstances supports my contention that there are no *a priori* limits that can be place on the use of picture books to initiate discussions of difficult philosophical topics with young children.

Notes

1 One of the anonymous readers suggested that I mistakenly assume that picture books can be used to discuss only one philosophical issue. He mentions that he led two discussions of *Where the Wild Things Are* with quite different foci. One discussed the justification of different types of punishment, while the other focused on the distinction between reality and dreams. In response, I would first note that I have never maintained that a picture book can only be used to discuss one philosophical issue. Anyone familiar with my website teachingchildrenphilosophy.org will know that there are a number of different philosophical issues associated with each picture book on the site. The fact that *Where the Wild Things Are* can be used to discuss different topics reflects the fact that these topics are raised by the book's narrative. I don't think this is the case with *Elmer* and race.

2 For reasons I don't understand, Chetty talks of reading against *the text*. I will follow the more traditional usage.

3 This book can be seen as critiquing Hegel's account of the life-and-death struggle in his *Phenomenology of Spirit*. According to Hegel, such battles result in a victor who becomes the lord over the vanquished warrior who becomes his slave. Interestingly, such wars are for Hegel the origin of slavery. McKee sees war as having no winners or losers, since everyone dies.

4 I don't mean to deny that it is not possible to discuss race using either *Elmer* or *Tusk Tusk*. I am just concerned that the results of such discussions will be as problematic as Chetty claims.

5 I leave aside the question of the validity of Murris' critique of Lipman. It may apply more to his early novels like *Harry* than to later ones like *Kia and Gus*.

9

HOW TO FACILITATE DISCUSSIONS
OF BOOKS WITH MORALS

In Chapter 7, I argued that the crux of a philosophical discussion of a picture book was transitioning from a discussion of the book's narrative to a consideration of the main concepts placed under scrutiny by the book. Such conversations, though grounded in the narrative, move from the specifics of the narrative to a more abstract discussion of the viability of the claims made by the book.

Bearing this in mind provides the key to clearing up a puzzle facing the facilitator of philosophy discussions based upon children's books. Many children's books *moralize*, that is, attempt to teach children a lesson. I refer to such books and stories as *fables*, a term derived from Aesop's *Fables*, all of which have a moral attached to them.

Consider, for example, Aesop's fable, "The Hare and the Tortoise." In response to the hare's making fun of him for being so slow, the tortoise proposes a race, much to the amusement of the hare. So overconfident is the hare that he decides to take a nap. The plodding tortoise passes the sleeping hare and wins the race. The fable ends with the following moral: "The race is not always to the swift."

Given the presence of a specific moral at the end of a fable like this one, it might seem impossible to base a philosophy discussion upon one. The story's concluding moral seems to usurp the possibility of discussing the story. It's meaning has been given in the text through the concluding moral.

But the presence of explicit morals does not undermine the possibility of having stimulating discussions of fables with children. In order to do so, one has to move away from the text itself and interrogate the plausibility of the moral and the adequacy of the stories' "big ideas."

DOI: 10.4324/9781003257455-12

9.1 Fables

Fables are stories, usually short, that have a specific moral. I have just presented one example: Aesop's fable of the Hare and the Tortoise. Most fairytales, the sorts of stories collected by the Brothers Grimm, are fables in just this sense, even when they don't make their moral explicit, as Aesop did. I will characterize certain picture books as fables in so far as they involve simple, decontextualized stories that attempt to convey a moral. Examples include *Elmer* and *Tusk Tusk*, books that I discussed in Chapter 8. Some novels for adults might even qualify, though they are not relevant to our discussion here.

The issue fables raise is how to have a genuinely philosophical discussion of one given that it contains its own moral, presents the message it wants to convey to its readers. The sorts of discussions we have with elementary-school children have a very different character, for they focus on issues for which there are at least two different sides. You'll recall that while discussing "Dragons and Giants," I asserted that it presented a counter-example to the claim that brave people never feel fear. Without getting into the details of how the story presents its counter-example, it is possible to have a philosophical discussion by asking children whether they think that a brave person can be scared. There are clearly two different possible responses to this question, so that the children are able to take a side and find reasons to support it. This, in essence, is what a philosophical discussion requires.

For example, one student might say that, as the story shows, you can be brave and still experience fear. After all, Frog and Toad are brave but they certainly were scared on their trip up the mountain. Another student might disagree, saying that brave people cannot feel fear, because if they did, they would be unable to respond adequately to the dangerous situation they face. Given the possibility of embracing either of these two different positions, the story can generate an interesting philosophical discussion about the relationship between fear and bravery.

The crucial feature of philosophical discussions is that they require students to make up their minds about issues that are contested, have two different sides to them. The issues do not have to be ethical ones, though there are many ethical issues that are appropriate topics for philosophical discussions in elementary schools. For example, young students enjoy discussing the question of whether it is possible to tell that one is not now dreaming. It has also been a philosophical issue since at least the time of Descartes, who thought that there was no intrinsic criterion that could distinguish a dream from reality. This issue falls within the field of epistemology, the area of philosophy dealing with knowledge, and is one students are really engaged by.

Despite appearances, stories with a clear moral can be used as the basis for philosophical conversations, though the facilitator needs to be creative. To demonstrate how this is done, I am going to look at one of the most famous and beloved fairytales of all time, "Cinderella." The story appears in many collections of fairytales, such as that of the Grimm Brothers, and has been retold in countless different ways.

An interesting feature of the fable is the parallel it presumes, at least in some versions, between a person's physical appearance and their moral character. In the story, Cinderella is a morally good person. She is also beautiful. Her step-sisters are evil, and hence are ugly.[1] This is established in the very first paragraphs of Charles Perrault's version from 1697:

> Once there was a gentleman who married, for his second wife, the proudest and most haughty woman that was ever seen. She had, by a former husband, two daughters of her own, who were, indeed, exactly like her in all things. He had likewise, by another wife, a young daughter, but of unparalleled goodness and sweetness of temper, which she took from her mother, who was the best creature in the world. No sooner were the ceremonies of the wedding over but the stepmother began to show herself in her true colors. She could not bear the good qualities of this pretty girl, and the less because they made her own daughters appear the more odious.

I want to emphasize how, in short compass, the fable establishes the existence of a correspondence between physical appearance and moral character. The good Cinderella is beautiful, while the evil of the two step-sisters is registered in their ugliness, as if the characters' physical appearance was a code for their moral character.

This parallel between physical appearance and moral character forms the background for the narrative of Cinderella's ill-treatment by her step-family and her rescue by Prince Charming. That is, it structures the narrative without itself being an element in it. Narratively, Cinderella's beauty is important, for although her step-family treats her badly, the Prince restores Cinderella to her rightful place by recognizing her beauty and, hence, moral worthiness. The moral of this fable is that goodness will triumph over evil and be rewarded, a moral that many people would like to believe is true.

There are many different topics to discuss in relation to "Cinderella." But it might not be apparent where to begin since the story ends with the conclusion that virtuous behavior will be rewarded with happiness. Many philosophers have believed this to be true, among them Immanuel Kant who thought that, without the prospect of happiness, morality would not be able to motivate people.

One can make this issue—whether being good will inevitably be rewarded with happiness—the topic of a philosophical discussion. One might start by asking the children to think of examples in which a good person was rewarded for a good act or a bad person was punished for an evil one. You could then ask them for examples in which a good person was wrongly accused or a bad one got away with something. They might tell the story of someone who cheated on a test but got away with it, for example, to show that a person who acts immorally will necessarily suffer as a result of their actions.

If the children agree that being good does not necessarily result in a reward and being bad does not inevitably bring punishment in its wake, the facilitator could then raise the more abstract, philosophical question of why one should act morally if it doesn't necessarily "pay." This is an important philosophical question and the path from "Cinderella" to it is quite easy to follow.

An alternate route that a philosophical discussion might take focuses on an assumption that forms the taken-for-granted background of the story. One of the most important background assumptions of "Cinderella," as I have shown, is that there is a strong correlation between physical appearance and moral character: good people are beautiful while evil people are ugly. In the story, only the female characters are described this way, opening the door to another possible discussion topic. But let's focus on this parallelism for now.

The facilitator might begin the discussion by saying something like this: "In this story, the evil step-sisters are ugly, while the virtuous Cinderella is beautiful. Do you think that this is true, that good looking people are morally superior to people who are not as good looking?"

A first thing to note is that when students are asked to consider the validity of the parallel between physical appearance and moral character, they won't be focusing on the tale's narrative but rather upon one of the background assumptions that lies behind it. In this way, the discussion is not limited by the point of view of the story's author, allowing for a richer discussion to take place.

But reflecting on the appearance–character parallel opens up aspects of the fairy-tale to critical discussion. In particular, it asks the students to consider whether this parallelism is true or not. It lets issues of feminism and standards of female beauty emerge. This allows the students to form a critical opinion about the fairy tale without having to counter its explicit message about the reward of being good.

So, even though "Cinderella," like many fables, comes with a clear moral, it is possible to use the story as the basis for a philosophical discussion. By investigating some of the assumptions behind the tale's narrative and assessing their validity, one can use fairytales as effective prompts for philosophical discussions.[2]

9.2 Moralizing Picture Books

Picture books can also qualify as fables in the sense of the term I am using. We therefore would do well to consider whether this presents an obstacle to basing philosophical discussions on books that have a moral rather than ones like "Dragons and Giants" that problematize philosophical issues.

In order to show that this is indeed possible, I will first turn to Harry Allard and James Marshall's 1977 picture book, *Miss Nelson is Missing!* This book has a distinctive moral even if it is only implicit. But it also presents the opportunity for an interesting discussion of an important moral issue: can deception ever be justified?

Miss Nelson is a school teacher who has an incredibly unruly class. Nothing she does can get them to pay attention. They continue to act up no matter what she does to try to get them to behave and do their school work. One day, Miss Nelson does not come to school. In her place, Miss Viola Swamp appears. Whereas the blonde Miss Nelson was sweet and kind, the black-haired Miss Viola Swamp wears "an ugly black dress" and is a tyrant in the classroom. (I leave aside here the book's correlation of goodness and colors, certainly a problematic feature of it.) But the children listen to her and do the work she assigns them. She gives lots of homework and gets the children to behave.

As a result of being terrified of Miss Viola Swamp, the children begin to miss Miss Nelson and start searching for her. They worry that she might have suffered some sort of attack. They try to get a police officer to help them find her, but he is no help. They speculate about what happened to Miss Nelson, inventing far-fetched stories to account for her absence. They begin to doubt she will ever return.

Suddenly, just as unexpectedly as when she disappeared, Miss Nelson reappears. The children are thrilled. She won't tell them where she was. But in one of the book's final spreads, we read that she hung her dress next to "an ugly black one," revealing that Miss Nelson and Miss Viola Swamp are one in the same. Miss Nelson created Miss Viola Swamp to get her class under control and she certainly succeeded in doing so, for the students now listen to her and do what she asks of them even though Miss Viola Swamp is long gone.

Particularly because of its surprise ending, *Miss Nelson is Missing!* presents Miss Nelson as having come up with a clever solution to her problem managing her classroom. Miss Viola Swamp's impact on the students is deep and lasting, for they continue to behave well even when the lovely Miss Nelson has returned.

What is the message *Miss Nelson is Missing!* seeks to impart? Since it is not explicitly stated in the book, it will be subject to interpretation and there can be disagreement about what the message really is. I think it is clear, however, that the book presents Miss Nelson's deception of her students—not telling them that she is not going to come to school one day and not revealing that Miss Viola Swamp is no other than herself, among other things—as justified by her inability to control them using normal classroom management techniques. The idea conveyed by both is that misbehavior can bring about a very unfortunate situation, so it is in the interest of the students to act in ways their teacher suggests.

The question that will allow for a stimulating discussing on this book is whether deception can ever be morally justified. As a first step, you might ask the children to say what they think Miss Nelson's justification for deceiving the students in her class is. Although students may respond to this question is different ways, one prominent answer is a *consequentialist* one: deceiving the students is justified because it results in improving their behavior.

Consequentialism is the ethical theory (or range of theories) uses an action's consequences to assess its morality. It claims that actions are justified so long as they increase the overall welfare more than any available alternative. Miss

Nelson has tried everything she can think of to get her class to behave prior to adopting the deceptive strategy of becoming Miss Viola Swamp. None of those actions actually improve the behavior of her class. But after her deception, the students act more respectfully and listen to what she says. This action is clearly the one that results in the greatest level of improvement in the behavior of her students and, hence, is morally justified from a consequentialist point of view.

A disagreement may arise if one or more students claim that it is simply wrong to deceive people. The philosophical rationale for this point of view stems from Kantian moral theory. Immanuel Kant (1724–1804) argued that moral actions could not violate the autonomy of individuals. People were, according to Kant, "ends in themselves," meaning that it was wrong to treat them merely as "means."

Students who say it was wrong for Miss Nelson to deceive her students would likely be taking a Kantian position, albeit without knowing that this is what they were doing. They might argue that Miss Nelson was not respecting the inherent dignity of every human being—another Kantian formulation—by not telling them the truth. Using deceit to improve the atmosphere of her classroom is not a justifiable course of action on this view.

So, despite the presence of a moral in *Miss Nelson is Missing!*, it is possible to conduct a discussion based on the book that raises an important philosophical issue. (By the way, there may be other issues as well. I am only discussing the one that struck me most forcefully and that links up to a fundamental issue in ethical theory.) The question of the morality of deception moves quickly into a conversation about morality more generally, as the arguments about deception's justifiability are based on more general moral principles as I have indicated.

There are many other moralizing picture books that can also result in fruitful philosophical discussions. *The Berenstain Bears* is a book series that is notable for the presence of a moral in every story. A good example is *The Berenstain Bears and the Truth* by Stan and Jan Berenstain (1983). Sister and Brother Bear are alone in the house and trying to find something to do. Brother Bear kicks a soccer ball at Sister who deflects it. Unfortunately, the ball breaks Mama Bear's favorite lamp. When she returns home, Brother and Sister Bear lie to her, telling her that a bird broke the lamp. They repeat the lie to Father Bear when he returns a little bit later, but they get confused about some of the details, such as exactly what color the bird was. As a result, they confess to what happened, with each of them taking the lion's share of the blame. Mama Bear is not angry because she says the two of them have learned an important lesson. The book ends with a recital of its moral: "But they never, ever again told a whopper because trust is one things you can't put together again once it's broken."

Like all the books in the series, *The Berenstain Bears and the Truth* has a moral that is clearly stated in the book. The two young bears lie and then realize that they shouldn't. And the book ends up providing an explicit moral that represents the learning process that the two bears experienced. The question that a book like this raises is whether it is possible to use it to begin a philosophical discussion.

One nice feature of the book is that it doesn't just provide a moral such as lying is wrong, it also provides a rationale for that claim. The book points out that telling a lie can result in the breakdown of trust between the person telling the lie and the one being lied to. The young bears expect their Mama to be angry with them, but she isn't. She explains that she's not worried about the lamp, because it can be replaced. What concerned her was that her cubs, whom she had always trusted, weren't telling her the truth. She concludes, "And truth is not something you can put back together again."

An easy place to begin a discussion of the book is with its moral. The facilitator might ask the children why the book says that telling a lie is a bad thing to do. This is what is called a *closed* question because it has a correct answer that can be found in the book. As I've just pointed out, the book explicitly links the prohibition on lying to the claim that discovering that you have been lied to can result in a breakdown of trust between you and the person telling the lie.

But reproducing the book's rationale for not lying is just the beginning of a discussion. The facilitator might follow up by asking questions about trust: what exactly is trust? Do you think that trust is important in a family? at school? Why or why not? What happens when someone you love no longer trusts you? Does telling a lie have to result in the breakdown of trust?

Here, you can see that the presence of a moral does not entail that the book cannot be used to generate a philosophical dialogue. All the facilitator needs to do is to use the moral as the starting point for a discussion that, rather than calling into question the moral—no one would presumably argue that lying is a good thing— takes off from the moral to ask other, fundamental philosophical questions.

There are many different tacks that the facilitator can use to have a philosophical discussion based on this book. In addition to the one I have just outlined, they could begin by asking the children, "Do you think it is every appropriate to tell a lie?" Although the children might initially deny that lying is ever justified, they are likely to subsequently realize that there are certain circumstances in which lying seems legitimate. The most obvious example is the "death-bed lie." Although I discussed this example earlier, it bears repeating again. The scenario here is that your good friend is dying and asks you a question, such as, "Did you remember to return the book to the library like I asked you?" Say that you forgot and you realize that telling your friend will cause her a great deal of anguish. If you lie to her and tell her that you returned the book, you will spare her a great deal of pain. Since she is dying, she won't have the opportunity to discover you were lying and so there are no possible negative consequences to your lying to her, only the positive one of sparing your friend unnecessary pain. In such circumstances, isn't it all right to lie to your friend?

The morality of white lies is a topic about which philosophers have had real disagreement, so that it is a good topic for an elementary-school philosophy discussion. From a consequentialist point of view—a theory I introduced during our discussion of *Miss Nelson*—the death bed lie is perfectly justified because it avoids unnecessary suffering and reasons along the lines that I have so far. The philosopher Immanuel Kant, whom we also met during the discussion of *Miss Nelson*, thought that telling the truth was always morally required. His idea was essentially Mama Bear's: discovering that one has been lied to will undermine one's trust that people will tell the truth, leading to a breakdown in our trust for one another. As a result, Kant denied that lies of any type could be justified.

The important takeaway from this discussion is that there are no picture books that cannot be used by creative facilitators to initiate philosophical discussions. With books that have explicit or even implicit morals, one has to avoid simply asking students whether they agree with the book or not, for they may not be in a position to debate what the book has claimed to be true. But with a bit of care, the facilitator is able to focus the discussion on other, related philosophical issues that can give rise to excellent philosophical conversations.

9.3 Conclusion

This chapter has focused on the question of whether stories with definite morals—what I have termed "fables"—can be used as the basis for philosophical discussions. Although focusing on the morals of such stories makes it hard to see how to generate the controversies necessary for philosophizing, I have shown that there are other features of the stories that can be used to ground discussions of important philosophical issues.

Notes

1 The Perrault version is explicit about Cinderella's beauty and the step-sisters ugliness: "However, Cinderella, notwithstanding her coarse apparel, was a hundred times more beautiful than her sisters, although they were always dressed very richly." In the Grimm Brothers version, this is not the case: "This wife [Cinderella's step-mother] brought two daughters into the house with her. They were beautiful, with fair faces, but evil and dark hearts." I will rely on the Perrault version for my discussion. If one used the Grimm Brothers' version, the discussion would take a different form.

2 Wendy Turgeon's *Philosophical Adventures with Fairytales* (2020) describes how to use a wide range of fairytales as the basis for philosophical discussions.

10

CONCLUSION

10.1 My Aims

I had two aims in writing this book. The first was to make the best possible case for why it's important to introduce philosophy to young children. I made this case in the first section of the book by presenting a number of different rationales for doing philosophy with children in Chapters 2 and 3. I began with the standard view that doing philosophy would make children better citizens because they learned how to assess arguments and to think for themselves. I supplemented this with a number of rationales that had not, to my knowledge, been offered previously.

I discussed how children's self-esteem was enhanced through a process in which they were asked to express their own opinions about important issues. Generally, children are not asked by the teachers to say what they think. When we do so in our philosophy discussions, the children come away with a sense that their views matter.

I also reiterated a theme I have sounded before: children are natural-born philosophers. The idea is that children, in encountering the world for the first time, naturally raise questions about its nature, the very questions that the first Greek philosophers, the Pre-Socratics, also asked. As a result, I argued, children deserve the opportunity to have their own questions discussed in schools. Having them take part in philosophical dialogues is one way to do that.

I then considered an innovative idea that one of the teachers we worked with told us about, viz. that children learned a method of dispute resolution from taking part in philosophical dialogues. That teacher's comments highlighted an important aspect of our practice: we teach children how to conduct a discussion in which there are opposing points of view without demeaning

DOI: 10.4324/9781003257455-13

any of the participants. The teacher pointed out that the children were able to apply some of the principles they learned from our philosophy discussions to their own disputes on the playground. This is an important benefit of doing philosophy that I do not believe has been acknowledged previously, that the methods for dispute resolution the children learn by participating in philosophical discussion can be transferred successfully to other arenas.

The final reason I presented for doing philosophy with children stems from their capacity for wonder. Although other practitioners mentioned children's wonder as a unique feature of this life-stage, they had not connected that capacity to the importance of introducing them to philosophy. Philosophers going all the way back to Plato claimed that philosophy itself began from the experience of wonder. What has been less widely acknowledged is how fragile that sense of wonder is, how liable to being diminished through the process of maturation. Taking part in philosophy discussions allows children to retain their sense of wonder at the features of the world and their own experience. I see this as one of the most important reasons to introduce them to philosophy.

The second aim I had in writing this book was to show that picture books were an effective vehicle initiating philosophical dialogues and I began to address this issue in the second section of *Thinking Through Stories*. There has been debate among practitioners of p4/wc about whether it is appropriate to use picture books in this way. To justify my view, I took a careful look at an alternative methodology, that of using philosophical novels written expressly for the purpose of classroom philosophical discussions. I showed that, even though there are advantages to using such novels, they also have serious problems stemming from the manner in which they incorporate philosophical theories in their narratives.

I then contrasted philosophical novels with picture books, arguing that commercially produced picture books had many advantages as stimuli for philosophical discussions. Most centrally, children become very engaged when they read or are read a picture book. This fuels their enthusiasm for philosophical discussions. This is due not only to the wit and humor so evident in picture books but also to the children realizing that the problems these literary works raise are ones that they had already been puzzled about in the course of living their lives. Arnold Lobel's Frog and Toad story "Cookies" provided me with a good example of how a story in a picture book raises an issue that is an important philosophical one but also one that children find themselves puzzled over in the course of their development.

The final chapter of this section made the case for recognizing that picture books have greater philosophical capacities than people generally acknowledge. Using another Frog and Toad story, "Dragons and Giants," I demonstrate how the story actually does philosophy by presenting a counter-example to a philosophical claim made in it. As a result, the story presents an excellent example for children of what a philosophical argument looks like, even though it is presented narratively in the story. I go on to show that the story also provides a corrective to popular cultural images of bravery that can be quite destructive in their effects. In both of these respects, picture books are capable of doing a lot more than people generally acknowledge and that these achievements justify using them as the basis for philosophical discussions.

The third and final section of this book addresses specific issues about the use of picture books to prompt philosophical discussions. I began with an issue that has troubled the p4/wc movement for years: how much philosophy does a facilitator need to know in order to be an effective facilitator of philosophical discussions using picture books? Although having acquaintance with philosophy certainly is beneficial for a facilitator, I don't think this means that someone without prior knowledge of philosophy cannot be a good philosophical facilitator. While they do need to be able to distinguish philosophical issues from other ones, that is something they can learn to do without having to, say, become a philosophy major in college. There are many ways to acquire the necessary philosophical background and I suggest what some of them are. I also outline the method we use to discuss picture books with elementary-school children.

Because picture books generally have simple narratives, some practitioners have argued that they cannot convey the complexity required for an adequate discussion of difficult issues. In particular, they have claimed that picture books present an abstract and a-historical understanding of race and racism, making it impossible to convey to children the structural features that have allowed racism to "flourish." Although I acknowledge that this is a genuine issue, I suggest that it only entails the need for exercising a great deal of careful thinking when selecting the appropriate book to use as a stimulus for a philosophical discussion of a difficult topic. I consider two recent picture books that present interesting and provocative stories about racism and that would be excellent ones to use to foster a discussion of this difficult topic. Both of these books focus on actual historical events having to do with racism and this makes them appropriate to use as stimuli.

A related problem is that many picture books are fables, that is, stories that come with a built-in message, such as "beauty is in the eye of the beholder." Although it might seem that the presence of explicit morals would make it difficult to have the sorts of open-ended discussions needed for philosophy, I argue that this is not the case, that it is perfectly possible to raise philosophical questions based upon a fable. Although this might require some more ingenuity on the part of the facilitator, it does not amount to a reason to avoid picture books in elementary-school philosophy classes. In fact, the very presence of a moral makes the question of its truth one point of entry for a philosophical discussion.

10.2 Alternative Methodologies

The emphasis this book places on "thinking through stories" may have given a mistaken impression of the methods that can be used to teach young children philosophy by focusing only on those that employed stories as prompts. I will now correct that impression by acknowledging that there are a variety of other ways to introduce philosophy into elementary-school classrooms.

To begin, we should note that *thought experiments* form a crucial aspect of philosophical argumentation. In a thought experiment, a hypothetical case is put forward for people to consider and respond to. The idea is that the thought experiment functions as, in the words of Daniel Dennett, an "intuition pump," something to provoke reflection on an important philosophical issue.

One of the most famous thought experiments in the history of Western philosophy is René Descartes' Evil Genius one. Toward the end of his first *Meditation on First Philosophy*, Descartes asks readers to imagine an Evil Genius who devotes all of his energy to deceiving them. When they think that they are seeing a blue sky overhead, there really is none there; the Evil Genius has just placed into their minds the perception of a blue sky overhead without there being a real object that corresponds to that perception. Descartes' claim is that it is possible for us to have all of the subjective experience we do have without the objective world actually existing in the manner specified by our perceptions of it.

A thought experiment like this is a good means of provoking a philosophical discussion because there are at least two plausible responses to it. One accepts Descartes' argument and tries to supply reasons for the validity of Descartes' claim. It might rehearse his argument based on the fact that he has been subject to deception in the past, so there is no way to tell that he is not now being deceived as well. Therefore, the Evil Genius hypothesis is based on his previous experience of deception and his inability to recognize the factors responsible for it.

The other response rejects Descartes' argument. There are a variety of different tacks that could be taken to support this point of view. Descartes' famous claim, "I think, therefore I am," was intended by Descartes in part to show that the Evil Genius hypothesis fails, for the Evil Genius cannot deceive Descartes—or anyone—about their own existence. Whenever one says, "I exist," Descartes claims, they can be certain of its truth, so the universal deception posited by the Evil Genius hypothesis cannot actually happen.

All this suggests that one can use thought experiments, many of them actually occurring in the history of Western philosophy, to get children to have a philosophical discussion. The thought experiment just needs to be presented clearly so that the children can understand it. There's no need, incidentally, to mention its source, which might only intimidate the children. But the facilitator needs to understand at least some of the possible responses so that they can help the children begin their discussion.[1]

One problem with using thought experiments with very young children is that they may not be prepared to discuss them in the manner that is necessary for having a philosophical dialogue with their classmates. A child needs to already have a sense of what is involved in a philosophical dialogue in order to take part in the discussion of a thought experiment such as the Evil Genius hypothesis. A child who has had no experience thinking about philosophical issues may find a thought experiment too difficult to respond to, thus making them reluctant to engage further in philosophical dialogues.

One reason why I am so passionate in my advocacy for using picture books is that they are a good way to *introduce* young children to philosophy and how to have a philosophical discussion. Particularly stories that model a philosophical discussion, such as virtually all of Arnold Lobel's Frog and Toad stories, are helpful in this regard because children can take from the characters' interactions an initial understanding of how to take part in a philosophical discussion.

Because so much of philosophy is a reflection on our everyday experience, there are many other strategies for getting children to take part in philosophical discussions. I have often pointed out that a facilitator could just empty their pockets and put all the objects that were in them onto a table or desk so that the children can see them. They could then ask the children what all the objects have in common. This will initiate a *metaphysical* discussion about different properties that those objects possess.

An obvious property that all the objects possess is that they were in the facilitator's pocket. But obvious as the property is, it is not a very interesting one. It is a *relational* property of the objects in question and is not based on their actual natures as the objects that they are. It is likely that most of the objects from one's pockets will be *artifacts*, that is, objects that were created by humans to satisfy specific needs, such as a key or a coin. There may also be some *natural objects*, say a piece of fruit or a rock. If that's the case, then there is the possibility of the children discussing what the difference is between the objects and whether there is any overarching characteristic that they all share. In so doing, they will be discussing *metaphysics*.

To lead such a discussion, the facilitator needs to have some background in metaphysics, the philosophical field that reflects on the underlying structure of the world and the entities in it. That's why I don't recommend that beginning facilitators use thought experiments: it would simply overwhelm them if they were not in possession of a reasonable understanding of the metaphysical issues at stake.

I have tried to explain why it is less important for a facilitator to have that knowledge when they are facilitating a philosophical dialogue based upon a picture book. The main reason is that the books themselves provide the context for the discussion, something that the facilitator can rely upon.

Whatever method a budding facilitator might choose to use, the fact that they are attempting to get children to engage in philosophical dialogues is what's important. The World Wide Web provides many resources that they can use to help them. I have mentioned my own website—teachingchildren-philosophy.org—as one that is particularly useful for discussions based upon picture books as well as the book I wrote—*Big Ideas for Little Kids*. The PLATO website (Plato-philosophy.org) has many other resources for individuals desiring to introduce philosophy to young people.

There are also many organizations across the globe that offer trainings for facilitators. These all can be traced back to the trainings that the IAPC has offered for many years. In these trainings, people are introduced to the basic principles for conducting philosophy discussions as well as to the practice of philosophy itself. These trainings are very useful for potential facilitators, but I've always been concerned about people who can't attend such trainings. Are they also able to learn how to facilitate philosophy discussions?

10.3 A Final Plea

The ultimate takeaway that I hope readers get from this book is that, however it is done, children deserve the opportunity to take part in philosophical dialogues. As natural-born philosophers, they are often preoccupied with questions that are inherently philosophical, even when the questions appear to have scientific answers. Because the world and their own selves are fresh and new to them, children find themselves confronted with phenomena that both amaze them and puzzle them. That is why *wonder* is such an important aspect of childhood. By introducing children to philosophy at an early age, we can help them preserve their sense of wonder at the mysteries of human existence and appreciate the possibility of coming to understand their own place in the world through talking about it with their friends and classmates.

Note

1 There are numerous books that present famous philosophical thought experiments. One I would recommend is Peg Tittle's *What If* (Routledge, 2004), a collection of 100 classical philosophical thought experiments.

APPENDIX: GLOSSARY OF PHILOSOPHICAL TERMS AND NAMES OF PHILOSOPHERS

1. Accident: see Essential property.
2. Aristotle (384–322 b.c.e.): The third of the great Greek philosophers. Aristotle was a scientist who studied many natural phenomena. He was incredibly influential, especially during the Middle Ages. His theories continue to be influential today.
3. Consequentialism is the ethical theory that bases the morality on its actual consequences. The most prevalent form of consequentialism is Utilitarianism, which holds that an action that promotes human happiness more than the other available options is moral.
4. Descartes, René (1596–1650): The "father" of modern Western philosophy, Descartes is known for making epistemology the basis for philosophy rather than metaphysics, as Aristotle had done. He is known for his methodological skepticism and his dualistic account of the human being.
5. *Deus sive Natura* (God or Nature): This phrase is used by Spinoza to characterize the one, infinite substance that he takes to constitute all of reality. This one substance has an infinite number of attributes according to Spinoza, of which we are aware of only two: mind and matter.
6. Dewey, John (1859–1952): The third great pragmatist philosopher after Charles Sanders Peirce and William James. Dewey's theories had a huge impact on American education. He was very concerned about the nature of education and founded the Laboratory School at the University of Chicago where he tested out his theories.
7. Dialogue: This term derives from Plato's written texts that featured discussions of philosophical topics between Socrates and a variety of interlocuters. Dialogues are face-to-face conversations among a number of

interlocuters. They tend to focus on a significant topic and feature inter-actions among the participants.

8. Dualism: The metaphysical theory that takes reality to be composed of two distinct substances, mind and matter. The central problem for this theory is that of interaction, i.e., how two distinct substances can affect one another. It is opposed to monism, the metaphysical theory that there is only one type of substance in the world. Monism can be either materialism or spiritualism, depending on the type of substance claimed to be the only one in reality.

9. Epistemology: The study of the nature and extent of human knowledge. Beginning with Descartes, it became the most basic of philosophical dis-ciplines. It focuses on the question of what humans are capable of know-ing and what limitations there might be to our knowledge.

10. Essential property: Aristotle distinguished between two types of proper-ties that objects possess. (A property is just a characteristic that an entity has.) An object's essential property or essence is the property that is pos-sesses that it cannot lose and still be the object that it is. For example, the essential property of a knife is its ability to cut things. An object that can-not cut is not a knife. Aristotle classified all the other properties of a thing as its *accidents* or accidental properties. These can change without affecting an object's nature. Having long hair is an accidental property of a human being, for they can go lose their hair without changing their nature.

11. Existentialism: The Existentialists are a loosely associated group of think-ers who emphasize the distinctive nature of human life or *existence*. They tend to treat the human being as different from all the other beings in the world in virtue of the fact that we are aware of ourselves, self-conscious. Existentialism flourish in France during and after World War II. The ideas of the Existentialists had a huge impact on popular culture through their literary and artistic creations as well as their philosophical texts.

12. Forms: In Plato's metaphysics, the Forms are the ultimate realities. Plato held that the objects that populate our world—tables, chairs, forks, knives, etc.—were appearances of a more fundamental reality, that of the Forms. The Forms were conceived of as eternal and unchanging, unlike ordinary things in our world that change and decay.

13. Heidegger, Martin (1889–1976): One of the central philosophers in the Existentialist movement. His major work is *Being and Time* (1927). In it, he develops an account of the experience of *Dasein*, his term for the human being. Heidegger thought that Western thought did not acknowl-edge the uniqueness of the human being. He is notorious for his support of the Nazi party and his anti-Semitism.

14. Heraclitus (c.535–c.475 b.c.e.): One of the most important pre-Socratic philosophers, he argued for the ubiquity of change. This view is encapsu-lated in his famous saying, "You cannot step in the same river twice. New waters are ever flowing."

15. Kant, Immanuel (1724–1804): Presented his "critical philosophy" in three *Critiques*, those of Pure Reason, Practical Reason, and Judgment. Central to his philosophy is the idea that we impose upon the given materials of the senses a set of categorial structures that can be known without reference to experience. His ethics emphasizes the notion of duty. Only those actions stemming from duty are moral according to Kant.

16. Metaphysics: The field of philosophy that specifies the nature of those things that exist. It is the most abstract area of philosophy.

17. Necessary condition: X is a necessary condition for Y just in case Y entails X. An example is lightning is a necessary condition for thunder. If there is thunder, you know that there must have been lightning. Cf. sufficient condition.

18. Nietzsche, Friedrich (1844–1900): One of the important precursors to Existentialism. Nietzsche saw Western civilization as having declined since its apex in Ancient Greece. He thought that there was hope for the dawning of a new age at the end of the nineteenth century. He advocated for the creation of a new type of human being, what he called the Overman (*Übermensch*), who would be capable of living a fuller life than that which his contemporaries did. He initially hailed the operas of Wagner as marking a high point in Western culture, but later broke with the composer over his anti-Semitism.

19. p4/wc: This term is an amalgam of p4c ("philosophy for children") and pwc ("philosophy with children") in an attempt to include all the various forms of pre-college philosophy.

20. Parmenides (late sixth, early fifth century b.c.e.): The great pre-Socratic philosopher who thought that ultimate reality could not be subject to change. He contrasted the way of being with the way on non-being, and also admitted a way of becoming that most humans accepted as reality.

21. Plato (428/7 or 424/3–348/7 b.c.e.): The second of the three great Ancient Greek philosophers, Plato is known for his theory of Forms. He wrote a series of dialogues that featured his teacher Socrates in conversation with a variety of speech partners. The early dialogues are thought to be an accurate representation of Socrates' intellectual practices, his trial for blasphemy, and his death. His middle and late dialogues develop and critique his theory of Forms.

22. Pragmatism: The school of philosophy that emphasizes the role of experience in generating questions for inquiry. The approach was developed by the nineteenth century American philosopher Charles Sanders Peirce and popularized by William James. It remains a distinctively American school of philosophy.

23. Princess Elizabeth of Bohemia (1618–1680): This noblewoman was interested in philosophy and conducted a correspondence with Descartes who served as her spiritual advisor as well as teacher. She objected to Cartesian

dualism on the grounds that it could not account for the interaction between two different types of substances. Descartes dedicated his work *Principles of Philosophy* (1644) to her.

24. Skepticism: Skepticism is a negative philosophy in so far as it denies the claims of another theory. Descartes, for example, developed a skeptical argument that denied the possibility of knowledge, although he later provided a means to refute it. Almost every philosophical position can be subjected to a skeptical challenge.

25. Slave morality: Nietzsche uses this term in his *Genealogy of Morals* to characterize our ordinary moral viewpoint. He claims that it arose from slaves' attempt to evade the power of their masters by labeling behaviors as *evil* that the masters disapproved of.

26. Socrates (469–399 b.c.e.): The first of the great Athenian philosophers. He did not write, but engaged in face-to-face philosophical dialogues with his fellow Athenians, some of which were recorded by his student, Plato, and provide a good picture of his practice. He got into trouble with the rulers of Athens and chose death over exile. He famously drank a cup of hemlock but continued to philosophize until his actual death.

27. Spinoza, Baruch (1632–1677): A Jewish philosopher who argued that there was only one existing substance, *Deus sive Natura* (see glossary entry). His philosophy was developed in response to Descartes. It avoided his dualism but only by denying that individual human beings count as substances. His major work, *Ethics*, emphasizes the importance of living a good life and holds out the promise of blessedness.

28. Sufficient condition: X is a sufficient condition for Y if X entails Y. Being a king is a sufficient condition for being a male. You can infer that someone is male from the fact that they are king. Cf. necessary condition.

29. Utilitarianism: The ethical theory of utilitarianism asserts that an action is moral only when it, more than any available alternative, promotes the general welfare. It was developed by Jeremy Bentham as a way to criticize his contemporary penal institutions. John Stuart Mill popularized the theory.

BIBLIOGRAPHY/WORKS CITED

Akeret, Julie. *Big Ideas for Little Kids: The Video.* Springfield, MA: WGBY, 2014. https://video.nepm.org/video/wgby-documentaries-big-ideas-little-kids/

Allard, Henry G., Jr. *Miss Nelson Is Missing.* New York: Houghton Mifflin Company, 1977.

Aristotle. *Nicomachean Ethics,* Terence Irwin, tr. Indianapolis: Hackett Publishing, 2000.

Augustine, Saint. *Confessions,* F.J. Sheed, tr. Indianapolis: Hackett Publishing, 2006.

Bagley, Jessica. *Boats for Papa.* New York: Roaring Brook Press, 2015.

Bartholomae, David, and Anthony Petrosky. *Ways of Reading: A Guide for Writers,* 12th ed. Boston and New York: Bedford/St. Martin's Press, 2019.

Bechdel, Alison. *Fun Home.* Boston and New York: Houghton Mifflin Company, 2006.

Berenstain, Stan and Jan. *The Berenstain Bears and the Truth.* New York: Random House, 1983.

Bernal, Martin. *Black Athena: The Afroasiatic Roots of Classical Civilization.* London: Free Association Books, 1987.

Brown, Margaret Wise. *The Dead Bird.* New York: Harper Collins, 1938.

———. *The Important Book.* New York: Harper Collins, 1949.

Celano, Marianne, Marietta Collins, and Ann Hazzard. *Something Happened in Our Town: A Child's Story about Racial Injustice.* Washington, DC: Magination Press, 2019.

Chetty, Darren. "The Elephant in the Room: Picturebooks, Philosophy for Children and Racism." *Childhood & Philosophy* 10, no. 19 (2014): 11–31.

Costello, Peter. *Philosophy in Children's Literature.* Lanham, MD: Lexington Books, 2013.

Cottingham, J., R. Stoothoff, and D. Murdoch. *The Philosophical Writings of Descartes,* Vol. 3. Cambridge, UK: Cambridge University Press, 1988.

de la Peña, Matt. *Last Stop on Market Street.* New York: G.P. Putnam's Sons, 2015.

Descartes, René. *Passions of the Soul,* Stephen H. Voss, tr. Indianapolis: Hackett Publishing, 1989.

———. *Meditations on First Philosophy,* Donald A. Cress, tr. Indianapolis: Hackett Publishers, 1993.

Fister, Marcus. *The Rainbow Fish.* New York: North South Books, 1992.

Gazzard, Ann. "Do You Need to Know Philosophy to Teach Philosophy to Children? A Comparison of Two Approaches." *Analytic Teaching and Philosophical Practice* 33, no. 1 (2012): 45–63.

Gopnik, Alison. *The Philosophical Baby: What Children's Minds Tell Us about Truth, Love, and the Meaning of Life*. New York: Farrar, Straus, and Giroux, 2009.

Grice, H.P. *Studies in the Way of Words*. Cambridge, MA: Harvard University Press, 1989.

Haynes, Joanna, and Karin Murris. *Picturebooks, Pedagogy, and Philosophy*. Abingdon: Routledge, 2012.

Hegel, G.W.F. *The Phenomenology of Spirit*, A.V. Miller, tr. Oxford: Oxford University Press, 1976.

———. *Hegel's Aesthetics: Lectures on Fine Art*, T.M. Knox, tr. Oxford: Oxford University Press, 1998.

Huget, Jennifer LaRue. "No Dinner for Max? It Depends on What He's Had to Eat." *The Washington Post*, November 8, 2011.

Johnson, Crockett. *Harold and the Purple Crayon*. New York: Harper Collins, 1955.

Kennedy, David. *My Name Is Myshkin: A Philosophical Novel for Children*. Münster, Germany: LIT Verlag, 2012.

———. *Dreamers: A Philosophical Novel for Children*. 2019. https://www.researchgate.net/publication/336312912_DREAMERS_A_Philosoph-ical_Novel_for_Children. Accessed July 31, 2021.

Kennett, Jeanette, and Michael Smith "Frog and Toad Lose Control." *Analysis* 56 (1996): 63–73.

Kidd, Kenneth B. *Theory for Beginners: Children's Literature as Critical Thought*. New York: Fordham University Press, 2020.

Kidder, Tracy. *Among Schoolchildren*. New York: Houghton Mifflin Company, 1989.

Kierkegaard, Søren. *The Journals of Kierkegaard*, Alexander Dru, tr. New York: Harper Collins, 1959.

Lipman, Matthew. *Harry Stottlemeier's Discovery*. Upper Montclair, NJ: The Institute for the Advancement of Philosophy for Children, 1971.

———. *Kia and Gus*. Upper Montclair, NJ: The Institute for the Advancement of Philosophy for Children, 1989.

Lipman, Matthew and Ann Margaret Sharp. *Wondering at the World: Instructional Manual to Accompany Kio and Gus*. Upper Montclair, NJ: Institute for the Advancement of Philosophy for Children, 1986.

Lipman, Matthew, Ann Margaret Sharp, and Frederick S. Oscanyan. *Philosophy in the Classroom*, 2nd ed. Philadelphia, PA: Temple University Press, 1980.

———. *Philosophical Inquiry: An Instruction Manual to Accompany "Harry Stottlemeier's Discovery."*, 2nd ed. Lanham, MD: University Press of America, 1984.

Lobel, Arnold. *Frog and Toad Together*. New York: Harper Collins, 1979.

Matthews, Gareth B. "Going Beyond the Deficit Conception of Childhood: Thinking Philosophically with Children." In *Philosophy in Schools*, Michael Hand and Carrie Winstanley, eds, 27–40. London and New York: Continuum, 2008.

McCloud, Scott. *Understanding Comics: The Invisible Art*. New York: Harper Collins, 1993.

McKee, David. *Tusk Tusk*. New York: Harper Collins, 1978.

———. *Elmer*. New York: Harper Collins, 1989.

Mills, Charles. *The Racial Contract*. Ithaca, NY: Cornell University Press, 2014.

Mills, Claudia. "Slave Morality in 'The Rainbow Fish'." In *Philosophy of Children's Literature*, Peter Costello, ed, 21–40. Lanham, MD: Rowman and Littlefield, 2012.

Murris, Karin. "Posthumanism, Philosophy for Children, and Anthony Browne's Little Beauty." *Bookbird: A Journal of International Children's Literature* 53, no. 2 (2015): 59–65.

———. "The Philosophy for Children Curriculum: Resisting 'Teacher Proof' Texts and the Formation of the Ideal Philosopher Child." *Studies in Philosophy and Education* 35 (2016a): 63–78.

———. *The Posthuman Child: Educational Transformation through Philosophy with Picturebooks*. London and New York: Routledge, 2016b.

Perrault, Charles. *Tales of Times Past: The Fairy Tales of Charles Perrault*, Alex Lubertozzi, tr. Chicago: Top Five Books, 2020.

Piaget, Jean. *The Essential Piaget*, Howard E. Gruber and J. Jacques Voneche, eds. New York: Basic Book, 2007.

Plato. *The Republic*, G.M.A. Grube, tr. Indianapolis: Hackett Publishers, 1974.

Priest, Graham. *In Contradiction: A Study of the Transconsistent*. Oxford: Oxford University Press, 2006.

Prinz, Jesse. "How Wonder Works." Aeon, June 21, 2013. https://aeon.co/essays/why-wonder-is-the-most-human-of-all-emotions

Ravitch, Diane. *The Death and Life of the Great American School System: How Testing and Choice Are Undermining Education*. New York: Basic Books, 2010.

Sendak, Maurice. *Where the Wild Things Are*. New York: Harper Collins, 1963.

Silverstein, Shel. *The Giving Tree*. New York: Harper and Row, 1964.

Smith, Adam. "The History of Astronomy." In *Essays on Philosophical Subjects*, 1–124. Edinburgh: Basil, 1799.

Spiegelman, Art. *Maus*. New York: Pantheon Books, 1980.

Tittle, Peg. *What If? Collected Thought Experiments in Philosophy*. Abingdon: Routledge, 2004.

Tonatiuh, Duncan. *Separate Is Never Equal: Sylvia Mendez and Her Family's Fight for Desegregation*. New York: Harry N. Abrams, 2014.

Wartenberg, Thomas. *Big Ideas for Little Kids: Teaching Philosophy Through Children's Literature*. Lanham, MD: Rowman and Littlefield, 2009, 2nd edition, 2014.

———. "Wordy Pictures: Theorizing the Relationship between Image and Text in Comics." In *The Art of Comics: A Philosophical Approach*, Aaron Meskin and Roy Cook, eds, 87–104. Oxford, and Malden, MA: Blackwell, 2012.

———. *A Sneetch Is a Sneetch and Other Philosophical Discoveries: Finding Wisdom in Picture Books*. Malden, MA: Wiley-Blackwell, 2014.

Weinberg, Justin. "Types of Contributions to the Philosophical Literature." *Daily Nous (blog)*, February 6, 2021.

Williams, Steve. "From Harry Stottlemeier's Discovery: Chapter 5." n.d. https://p4c.com/wp-content/uploads/2016/03/RT-Harry-Stottlemeiers-Discovery.pdf

———. "Philosophical Dialogue with Children about Complex Social Issues: A Debate about Texts and Practices." *Childhood & Philosophy* 16 (2020): 1–28.

Wittgenstein, Ludwig. *The Philosophical Investigations*, G.E.M. Anscombe, P.M.S. Hacker and Joachim Schulte, tr. Malden, MA: Wiley-Blackwell, 2009.

Worley, Peter. *100 Ideas for Primary Teachers*. London: Bloomsbury, 2019.

INDEX

Page numbers followed by n denote notes.

abstraction/abstractness 54, 90–91
accidents 82–83, 113
achievement orientation of adults 26, 27, 30
adults: achievement orientation of 26, 27, 30; adult-centered ontology 90; and linguistic abilities 23–24, 47–48
African-American children 93–94
agenda setting 43
aging 25–26
Akeret, J. 15
Alice's Adventures in Wonderland (Tenniel) 52, 93
Allard, H. 102–103
analytic philosophy 45–46
Andrews, R. G. 37n4
anti-Mexican racism 95
appearances 4
Aristotelian treatises 45
Aristotle 17, 32, 69, 82–83,113
art and wonder 29
astonishment 31
Austin, JL 48
authenticity 88

Baker, J. L. 60n9
Bartholomae, D. 89
being at home in world 34
Ben-Day dots 54, 55
Berenstain, J. 104
Berenstain, S. 104

The Berenstain Bears and the Truth 104–105
bête noire 30
The Bible 54
Big Ideas for Little Kids: Teaching Philosophy Through Children's Literature (Wartenberg) 75, 84
Black Lives Matter Movement 94
bravery: exploring with Frog and Toad 61–65; a positive account of 70
Brothers Grimm 100
Brown, M. W. 18, 81
Brown vs. the Board of Education 95

Carle, E. 55
Cartesian dualism 14, 21n1
Celano, M. 94
Chapman and Hall 54
character traits 79
Chetty, D. 86–87, 90–96
children's acquisition of language 23
cognitive skills 53
"Comics" 54
concept map 76–77
concrete operational stage of childhood 25
conflict resolution, philosophy as a form of 19–20
consciousness 56–57
consequentialism 103–106, 113
continental tradition of philosophy 45–46
Corrupting Youth (Worley) 21n8
critical race theory 87
curricula, elementary-school 19, 23, 25

Daily Nous 68
Dante 54
The Dead Bird (Brown) 18
death 1-2,17–18, 97
deep listening 78
deficit model of childhood 23
de la Peña 93–94
Dennett, D. 110
Descartes, R. 2, 14, 30, 32–33, 100, 110, 113
Deus sive Natura 3, 113
developmental stages of childhood 24
Dewey, J. 3, 12, 113
dialogues 3, 5–6, 13–14, 20, 32, 36, 45–46, 68, 76–77, 89, 92, 113
Dickens, C. 54
distinctiveness 89
Divine Comedy (Dante) 54
Dr. Seuss (Theodor Geisel) 55, 60n7
"Dragons and Giants" 65–67
Dreamers (Kennedy) 46
dualism 14, 21n1, 114

elementary-school curricula 23, 25
Elisabeth, Princess of Bohemia 14, 115
Elmer (McKee) 87–89
emotions 28–29
empathy 24
enquiries 90
epistemology 90, 114
Eric Carle Museum of Picture Book Art 53
essence 82–83, 89
essentialism 82
essential property 82–83, 89, 114
ethical practices 42
ethical thinking 24
Evil Genius hypothesis 110
existentialism 114
existentialists 88

fables 100–102
facilitating discussions of books with morals: fables 100–102; moralizing picture books 102–106
facilitators 76–81; trainings for 112
facilitator of an elementary-school, knowledge of philosophy in: *The Important Book* 81–85; methodological background 76–81
fear 58, 62, 64–70
first-order logic 49
Fister, M. 88

formal operational stage of childhood 25
forms, Plato's theory of 4, 114
Fun Home (Bechdel) 54

Goering, S. 37n5
Goldberg, S. 67–68
Good Night Moon (Brown) 81
Gopnik, A. 26, 30, 34
Gorgias (Plato) 45
graphic novels 54
Greek philosophy 16
Grice, P. 48
Grimm Brothers 101, 106n1

Harold and the Purple Crayon (Johnson) 57
Harry Stottelmeier's Discovery (Lipman) 43, 46–50
Harvard Center on the Developing Child 23
Haynes, J. 52, 60n8, 90–91
Hegel, G. W. F. 32
Heidegger, M. 2, 18, 32, 114
Heraclitus 16, 72n2, 114
The History of Astronomy (Smith) 28–29

illustrated books, types of 53–55
illustrations 52–54, 77
imagination 53
impatience 79
The Important Book (Brown) 81–85
individuality 88, 89
infants 24
inquiry 80
Institute for the Advancement of Philosophy for Children (IAPC) 11, 43, 44
interpretation of the text 88–89

James, W. 3
Johnson, C. 57

Kant, I. 28, 101, 104, 106, 115
Kennedy, D. 46
Kennett, J. 35
Kidd, K. B. 45
Kierkegaard, S. 32
Kio and Gus (Lipman) 44

language: learning 26; linguistic abilities and adults 23–24, 47–48; philosophy 47–49

Last Stop on Market Street (de la Peña)
93–94
Lectures on Aesthetics (Hegel) 32
Leibniz, G. W. 14
Lionni, L. 55
Lipman, M. 8n1, 11, 15, 16, 25–26, 27,
41, 43–50, 51, 59, 75, 93
Lobel, A. 13, 34–35, 61–65, 78
Locke, J. 17
lying 105

Malebranche, N. 14
Marshall, J. 102–103
Massachusetts Curriculum Frameworks
51
Matthews, G. B. 23, 25, 41, 45, 51,
60n2
Maus (Spiegelman)
McKee, D. 86, 87, 98n3
Meditation on First Philosophy (Descartes)
2, 14, 110
metaphysics 32, 83, 115
Mills, C. 87, 88–89, 93
Miss Nelson is Missing! (Marshall and
Allard) 102–103
Modes of Thought (Whitehead) 32
moral character 101
moral theory 104
morality of white lies 105–106
moralizing picture books 102–106
Murris, K. 45, 52, 90–91, 92–93
Murris' critique of Lipman 98n3

National Geographic 21n6
necessary condition 65, 115
Nicomachean Ethics 69, 72n2
Nietzsche, F 88–89, 115

objective reality 75
Oscanyan, F. S. 52
The Other Side (Woodson) 92–93
Oxford Dictionary of the English Language
28

p4/wc 115
parallelism 102
Parmenides 16, 17, 115
The Passions of the Soul (Descartes) 32–33
patience 79
Peirce, C. S. 3, 80
Perrault, C. 101, 106n1
Petrosky, A. 89
Phenomenology of Spirit (Hegel) 98n3

Philosophical Adventures with Fairytales
(Turgeon) 106n2
philosophical discussions 78–81
The Philosophical Investigations
(Wittgenstein) 48
philosophical novels, uses and limitations:
philosophical novels for children
43–46; setting the agenda 41–43;
trouble with *Harry Stottelmeier's
Discovery* (Lipman) 46–50
philosophical reasoning 79
philosophy with children: introduction
in elementary-school classrooms
11–16; philosophy as a form of
conflict resolution 19–20; wrongness
in philosophy 13–16
Piaget, J. 22–23
Piaget's "Deficit" model of childhood
23–26
Pickwick Papers (Dickens) 54
picture books 34–35
picture books, advantages of: Lipman's
Argument 51–53; word and image in
Where the Wild Things Are (Sendak)
55–59; words and images in a picture
book 53–55
picture books and philosophical discussions: bravery, a positive account of
70; exploring bravery with Frog and
Toad 61–65; philosophy in "Dragons
and Giants" 65–67; responding to a
skeptical attack 67–69
picture books for discussing racial issues:
addressing race through picture books
93–95; *Elmer* 87–89; *Tusk Tusk* 90–92;
Williams on picture books 92–93
plagiarism 42
Plato 3, 17, 18, 20, 32, 45, 68, 69, 89,
115
Polemarchus 68
Popova, M. 37n1
pragmatism 45, 115
pre-operational stage of childhood 24
Pre-Socratics 16-17, 107, 114n14, 115n20
Prinz, J. 29–30
properties 82
puzzlement 31–32, 33

questioners, children as 27–28
questioning 31, 33–34

racial contract 87
The Rainbow Fish (Fister) 88–89

read-aloud 76–77
The Republic (Plato) 3, 68, 69
Russell, B. 47

self-consciousness 23–24
self-control 23
Sendak, M. 7, 51, 55–60
sensory-motor stage of childhood 24
*Separate is Never Equal: Sylvia Mendez
    and Her Family's Fight for Desegregation*
    (Tonatiuh) 95–96
Sharp, A. M. 16, 43, 52
skepticism 35–36, 116
slave morality 88, 116
Smith, A. 28–31, 32
Smith, M. 35
social specificity 91
Socrates 17, 18, 20, 32, 68, 89, 116
*Something Happened in Our Town: A
    Child's Story About Racial Injustice*
    (Celano et al) 94, 96
Spinoza, B. 2, 14, 116
stimulated imagination 53
sufficient condition 82, 115n17, 116
superficial characteristic 91

teachingchildrenphilosophy.org 76, 79
Tenniel, J. 52–53, 93
Theatetus (Plato) 32
Thinking (journal) 60n2
thought experiments 110–112
Tittle, P. 112n1
Tonatiuh, D. 95
Tractatus Logico-Philosophicus
    (Wittgenstein) 47
trust 105–106
truth 104

Turgeon, W. 106n2
Tusk Tusk (McKee) 86, 87, 90–92

Utilitarianism 116
The Universe in Verse (Ackerman) 22,
    37n1

verbal description of a character
    or event 55

Ways of Reading (Petrosky and
    Bartholomae) 89
What If (Tittle) 112n1
Where the Wild Things Are (Sendak) 51,
    55–59, 75
Whitehead, A. N. 32
white lies, 105–6
White supremacy 87
Williams, S. 46, 50n3, 92–93
will power 35–36
Wittgenstein, L. 47, 48
wonder, role in childhood 22–36;
    childhood and wonder 27–32; lack of
    49-50; philosophy, wonder, and
    children 32–34; Piaget's "Deficit"
    model of childhood 23–26; picture
    books 34–35, 60
Woodson, J. 92
words and images: in a picture book
    53–55; in *Where the Wild Things Are*
    55–59
Worley, P. 21n8
written text 54
wrongness in philosophy 13–16

A Year with Frog and Toad (Broadway
    musical) 61–65

Printed in the United States
by Baker & Taylor Publisher Services